Fact and Fancy in International Economic Relations

Fact and Fancy in

International Economic Relations

AN ESSAY ON INTERNATIONAL MONETARY REFORM

by

THOMAS BALOGH

in collaboration with

PETER BALACS

PERGAMON PRESS

Oxford · New York · Toronto · Sydney · Braunschweig

143915

Pergamon Press Ltd., Headington Hill Hall, Oxford
Pergamon Press Inc., Maxwell House, Fairview Park, Elmsford, New York 10523
Pergamon of Canada Ltd., 207 Queen's Quay West, Toronto 1
Pergamon Press (Aust.) Pty. Ltd., 19a Boundary Street,
Rushcutters Bay, N.S.W. 2011, Australia
Vieweg & Sohn GmbH, Burgplatz 1, Braunschweig

First edition 1973

Library of Congress Cataloging in Publication Data

Balogh, Thomas, Baron Balogh, 1905–
Fact and fancy in international economic relations.

'The text of this book is reissued from World
development, volume 1, February and March 1973.'
1. International economic relations.   2. International
finance.   I. Balacs, Peter, joint author.
II. Title.
HF1411.B24 1973   382.1   73–7993
ISBN 0–08–017740–9

Contents

Preface

HARDLY had the ink on the postscript to this essay dried (October 1972) than we were faced with two further currency upheavals within eighteen months of the *coup de dollar* in August 1971. The first of these provoked the third depreciation of the pound during its stint of 'dirty floating' and saw the downward slide of the lira through the floor of the 'snake in the tunnel'. This in turn was followed by a sharp attack on the dollar, apparently led by a combination of multi-national corporations and oil sheikhs, culminating in a second devaluation of the dollar in terms of gold, and the 'floating'—separately—of the yen and most of the European currencies. After a further small revaluation of the Deutsche Mark, it is now planned to maintain a fixed relationship between these currencies, but on the original basis of a $2\frac{1}{2}$ per cent band, rather than the $1\frac{1}{4}$ per cent 'snake'. The end of fixed parities was accompanied by a renewed bout of self-congratulatory pronouncements, although this time around they were perhaps a shade more cautious compared with President Nixon's grandiloquent claim a year and a quarter earlier to have had the 'privilege of announcing the conclusion of the most significant monetary agreement in the history of the world'. The risks to export industries, the inevitable stimulus to speculative or 'precautionary' shifts of money, are ignored or minimized in this new euphoria. Yet what has happened must add further fuel to the inflationary spiral—not least in Britain. Indeed, second thoughts have been iterated before even first thoughts have been properly elaborated.

All these upheavals, which leave the great multi-national corporations, oil sheikhs and others who, whether legally or illegally, are able to move into Marks or yens many hundreds of millions of dollars the richer, contribute nothing to the better allocation of resources: they merely increase the risks facing export industries at a time when the very opposite is required. They certainly bring no economic enlightenment. Gone are the days when Keynes, to the approval of many, railed against the affairs and happiness of the world being entrusted to the tender mercies of a casino. Nowadays the financial directors of multi-national corporations are lauded for their skill in contributing by their activities to the destruction of the purchasing power of the reserves of poor countries. True enough, we are witnessing on the academic plane the disillusionment of those who used to be called 'elasticity optimists' after the war. After the National Institute's analysis of British experience since 1967[1] the enthusiasm, even of Cambridge,[2] for devaluation or downward floating as a smooth and effective instrument of balance-of-payments management has been on the wane. None too soon. The experience of the United States, following that of Britain, especially in the second half of 1972, vindicates a sceptical attitude. But the intellectual victory has not resulted in a change of policy. On the contrary, the world seems to be pressing on with the liberalization of short-term capital flows, despite their palpably destructive consequences.

It is more than doubtful whether Britain's difficulties will not be aggravated by the downward floating of the pound, as a result of the impact of the consequent deterioration in the terms of trade on the volume of available resources, and hence by the rise in prices and the resulting exacerbation of wage demands. Not only will this have the effect of sharpening class conflict at a highly explosive juncture; its implications for Britain will be even more acute especially now, for the reason that the costs of the C.A.P. and the E.E.C. budget are denominated in gold. On the other hand, however, a return to fixed parities and narrowed bands (e.g. 'the snake in the tunnel') might cause such a further deterioration in the balance of trade that, in the absence of a coherent incomes policy, defensive measures would have to be taken, leading inevitably to a severe increase in unemployment. Any direct American pressure for trade concessions following their exclusion from certain erstwhile E.F.T.A. markets—including Britain—might aggravate the British (and European) problem.

Even more ominous is the virtual abandonment of prices and incomes policy by the United States, despite its patent success. It is clear that both this and the promised phasing out of controls over, and taxation (in the form of the interest equalization tax) of, U.S. foreign investment have resulted from the extreme dogmatism of the Republican high command and their dissatisfaction with the success achieved by (in their opinion) 'unconformable' policies. Such a reaction will make it more difficult to adopt a rational approach to the basic problem of the Western system of international economic relations and threatens to throw the burden of adjustment on to its non-American partners. The fact that the Europeans—and in particular the Germans—have pressed for the lifting of controls over U.S. exports of capital shows how little progress has really been made since 1929 in applied economic analysis on the part of policy-makers. The fact is that

---

[1] See National Institute of Social and Economic Research, 'The effects of the devaluation of 1967 on the current balance of payments', *Economic Journal*, 82 (Mar. 1972), Supplement, pp. 463–4; also p. 60 below.

[2] See Cambridge Economic Policy Group, *Prospects for Economic Management* (University of Cambridge Department of Applied Economics, mimeo, Jan. 1973) chs. iii and iv, especially ch. iv, p. 15, para. 40.

the United States is perhaps the only single economy which, because of its size and natural self-sufficiency, needs to pay no attention to the impact of domestic economic problems on movements in the foreign exchanges. At the same time the United States is much the most important market for other people's products. This double advantage, so prominent after World War II, would undoubtedly be exploited again if put to the test once more now. President Nixon's threat to impose unilateral tariffs for the protection of exposed U.S. industries comes at a time when the whole structure of exchange rates has become unfixed. It is doubtful whether the revaluation of the yen and the Deutsche Mark will have the desired effect. The probability is that most European currencies will come under pressure from both Germany and the United States—while Japan will most probably drop its array of measures, weakly devised to hold back exports in most sensitive fields and markets. It is interesting and amusing to reflect once again that most orthodox economists do not regard devaluation as coming under the category of trade aggression. The only rational explanation of this is that most of them couch their discussions within a framework of static long-run adjustment and therefore cannot handle either the micro- or macro-problems which loom so large for the more rational observers.

The events of the last few weeks have amply confirmed my much ridiculed view[3] that the liberal international monetary system contains the seeds of its own undoing. Any national advantage, whether knowingly snatched or unwittingly come by, would accumulate of its own, and thus disrupt the even flow of trade; the weaker partner will then ultimately be forced to adopt policies that are inappropriate from its own domestic viewpoint. Continuous balance in international trade thus depends on its being consciously maintained through an appropriate policy on incomes and on adherence to certain rules of conduct, especially with respect to capital movements both long- and short-term—the theme of this essay. Events may now have come full circle and we may, if my forebodings about the possible failure of international monetary reform are justified, see the emergence of a dollar shortage and the forced liquidation of the overblown Euro-currency market—with all the potentially serious consequences that these would entail.

(1) What the extreme monetarists[4] choose to ignore is (a) that everybody cannot float downwards and (b) that there exists for most countries no such thing as an 'equilibrium' rate of exchange, because of the interconnection between domestic economic developments and international economic relations. According to our analysis in this essay downward exchange

---

[3]See G. D. N. Worswick (ed.), *The Free Trade Proposals* (Oxford: Blackwell, 1960).

[4]See, for example, *The Economist*, **246** (17 Feb. 1973) for an extreme and extremely ignorant and inconsistent statement of this case.

movements will probably give rise to secondary effects which will justify and, in turn, amplify the original movement.

(2) It is therefore a most dangerous illusion to imagine that a monetary union can be established in Europe by widening the band within which exchange rates can fluctuate—in other words by merely eliminating the 'snake' and maintaining the 'tunnel'. A much more coherent and far-reaching policy package is needed—but for this hardly any country in Europe is yet ready.

(3) The rise of multi-national firms has vitiated conventional notions about price formation, because a large proportion of foreign trade takes place in the form of transfers between interconnected firms or subsidiaries. A displacement of reserves or even a variation in leads and lags could decisively influence the overall balance of payments.

(4) For these reasons both long- and short-term capital movements must be controlled, whether such control take the form of blocking fluctuating balances or prohibitions on the acceptance of deposits.

(5) More particularly, the scandal of the wholly uncontrolled Euro-dollar market, which is the font of most of our troubles, must be ended. Reserve ratios for these deposits must be imposed multilaterally; and all central-bank lending of reserve (Euro-) dollars to anyone besides other central banks must cease.

(6) If the American administration insists on a turn-round in their current balance of payments large enough to be able to finance U.S. long-term capital investment abroad, i.e. to a very large extent the acquisition of existing assets rather than increasing physical investment capacity, then the surplus so achieved is likely not only to undermine the stability of the weakest economies, but also to exert a direct deflationary pressure all round. Given the vast disproportionality between the United States and the rest of the free world,[5] the danger of serious imbalance originating from this type of policy-atavism is grave.

(7) In particular, the pretence that such capital movements reflect 'social long-run rates of return' and that they therefore 'optimize' investment or 'world income' is ludicrous. The liberalization of capital exports now threatened by President Nixon and advocated by monetarists the world over will in all probability end in a repetition of the struggle for markets such as disfigured the inter-war period. We seem to have learned nothing from that disastrous experience nor from our relative good fortune since.

(8) A flexible funding of the outstanding key-currency reserve balances should be undertaken once the so-called Euro-dollar markets (which inflate them) have been brought under control.

---

[5]This problem was analysed in my essay 'The United States and the world economy', *Bulletin of the Oxford University Institute of Statistics*, 8 (Oct. 1946) pp. 309–23, reprinted in T. Balogh, *Unequal Partners*, 2 vols. (Oxford: Blackwell, 1963) ii, sect. 5, No. 12, pp. 149–59.

The scheme outlined in this essay is based on a modification of the S.D.R. system. Among its proposals is the establishment of an adjustable link between the creation of new reserves and development aid, but above all it is insisted that little can be achieved without the implementation of a strict code of conduct. Such an approach is unlikely to find favour among the ruling oligarchy, whether Gaullist, Christian Democrat or Social Democrat; the sway of the Quantity Theory of Money, despite its complete inability to offer a coherent account of what has actually happened, is uppermost. On the one hand, they fear inflation as being the consequence of an influx of liquid funds alone, funds which will hardly ever find their way into general circulation, but on the other hand are quite willing to abolish direct controls, the result of which might well be to force the countries of the world to adopt policies that in turn will lead inevitably to trade war.[6] I have little doubt that we are still far from a rational solution to the problem of creating a suitable instrument for international economic management in the field of monetary reform. Nor are the efforts of the Committee of Twenty likely to bring about any change in this gloomy prospect.

If the proof of the pudding is in the eating I need not be too dissatisfied. Even the Governor of the Bank of England—whose predecessors have contributed so much to Britain's eclipse—has now admitted that a grave problem exists in respect of the uncontrolled movement of hot money across national borders.[7] This was by far the most urgent of my conclusions, although the mere discussion of controls has hitherto been strictly taboo.

Recent events also have given strong support to my approach to the problem of international monetary relations, which is to treat it as a politically influenced, tactical oligopoly game. The 'undevaluable' dollar was devalued—or rather allowed to depreciate—thus confounding the financial commentators; but its relative stability thereafter has been entirely due to the unwillingness of her trading partners to permit any further improvement in the United States' competitive position.

---

[6]The recent liberalization of monetary management by the Bank of England shows equally an astonishing ignorance of the nature and functioning of oligopolistic markets, such as the capital and money markets are in highly developed countries. The demand for and supply of funds are controlled by a few leading firms which can match each other's moves. Non-interference merely results in the exaggeration of fluctuations and ultimately increases inflationary pressures, since under present circumstances increases in interest rates, as with other costs, will be shifted on to the consumer.

[7]In a lecture at Suerf, University of Nottingham, 11 April 1973.

President Nixon, although influenced by his own and his friends' reviving dogmatism into virtually abandoning domestic controls over prices and incomes, has since been forced by a renewed inflationary surge into reviving them.[8] His British counterpart, Mr. Heath, has had better luck with the unions, which seem tacitly or covertly willing to tolerate far more sensible policies under Tory sponsorship than those which they are dictating to the unfortunate Labour Party—this despite his disastrous financial policies, which have resulted in a formidable Budget deficit, increased inequality, and made a true recovery in the shape of an export-led expansion difficult if not impossible.

Finally my views have been fully vindicated in the emergence of the Deutsche Mark as a reserve currency.[9] This occurred without the 'happy coincidences' of an alteration in the rules of the I.M.F., which rules were thought by some authors to have been the reason for the predominance of the dollar. The outlook in the spring of 1973 thus remains sombre, with our independence from the follies of the banking fraternity as distant a goal as ever.

---

[8]The econometric jejuneness of the monetarist type, based inconsistently on the exploded Phillips curve, will be revealed by the impact of these political fluctuations on economic trends. The much-publicized £37,000 Manchester University project to discover the causes of inflation and its effects has, two years after its inception, run predictably into the sand.

[9]See p. 32, esp. note 17. According to *Le Monde* (25 April 1973, p. 25), of the DM54 billion in foreign exchange absorbed by the Bundesbank between 1970 and 1972 only DM5 billion was accounted for by the surplus on Germany's current account; the remainder represented an influx of unstable funds in the expectation of gain from yet a further revaluation. The Mark became the ultimate reserve currency for those free to take advantage of the 'freedom' to move capital about. Thus my analysis of the reasons for the rise of a *numéraire* being independent of the constitutional subtleties of the international monetary system has been fully borne out.

Acknowledgement

THE author would like to express his gratitude to the Social Science Research Council for providing the finance which made the present work possible and to Queen Elizabeth House, Oxford, where the bulk of the research was conducted, for offering its facilities. The essay which follows represents in part the results of a wider project concerning the impact of economic theory and government organization on economic policy-making.

Publisher's Note

THE text of this book is reissued from *World Development*, Volume 1, February and March 1973.

Notes to the textual references are printed on pages 87–112, and an indication of the pages on which the relevant note references occur appears in square brackets in the Notes page headlines.

1. Introduction

LIBERALS, and socialists even more so, have always found themselves in an awkward intellectual and moral position when it comes to the question of economic relations, whether between men or between countries. The cause of this lies in the obvious inequality of these relations, the imbalance of dominance and dependence which cannot be reconciled with the avowed abhorrence of both Christians and Radicals of the power of man over man, whether overt or concealed. This was especially the case in Victorian and Edwardian Britain which benefited most from such relations, not only through the lucrative, if morally distasteful, outlet which they secured for upper-class employment in her dependent areas (and not merely the colonies), but also from the support given to domestic incomes (including wages) as a result of the privileged treatment afforded to British exports and of her dominant position in commerce, shipping, insurance and other services.[1]

It is not surprising, therefore, that the classical and neo-classical theories of economics, as most vigorously developed in the Anglo-Saxon countries, should have found a way to disperse this atmosphere of ambivalence, moral abhorrence, and to resolve the ethical dilemma—particularly where it was most acutely felt, *vis-à-vis* their colonial territories—by justifying the existing political economy of the world. By claiming the existence of pervasive and impartial laws, to which all participants in the economic process are totally subject, it became possible to resolve all moral doubts. It followed from this claim that economic agents, acting individually in their own interests, could disregard the actions of others, even in the field of international relations; the outcome of their several endeavours, no matter what their private wills, would be ordained by the fusion of automatic motivations. No one, and no country, could then be accused of wielding discretionary power, despite all evidence to the contrary. What appeared to be domination could then be rationalized in terms of economic laws which not only could one single country bend to its advantage, but which worked unerringly in the direction of 'progress' through the 'optimal' allocation of resources and pattern of output. No direct moral responsibility or blemish could possibly attach to a mere executive of a higher will, whether in the domestic or international context.

1

The purpose of economic laws is not only to depersonalize, to create a determinate system in which everybody is absolved of *all* responsibility: they have also been used to prove the existence of a harmony of interests— or at least that there is a just distribution of the fruits of human toil. In a closed economy the latter aim was achieved in (or rather characterizes) the theory of perfect competition, as generalized in the Walrasian general equilibrium model with the help (at present) of either the Keynesian or the monetarist (Quantity Theory) explanations of the flow of money expenditure. In the international sphere this harmonious vision was completed by the addition of an only slightly modified model of international 'readjustment', based originally on relative movements in prices (and incomes) under the influence of 'specie flows'. These movements, which occur smoothly and automatically, are the net result, so to speak, of economic changes affecting myriad individuals.

Fashionably referred to as Hume's law (in imitation of the natural sciences—especially by American authors), this mechanism has been suitably remodelled since its formulation in the eighteenth century.[2] Even if, in stark contrast to the basic properties of the model, dynamic phenomena were admitted, either by way of an addendum or footnote, this harmony of interests was nonetheless regarded as inviolate. Technical progress, so it was held, would inevitably spread its beneficial effects through the fall in the price of industrial products whose production would so be stimulated. The price of agricultural products, on the other hand, would increase both relatively and even absolutely, by virtue of the law of increasing cost.[3] In this way the primary-producing countries also would derive part of the benefits of progress, that is, as a result of the improvement on their terms of trade.

Much the most important aspect of this model of harmony, however, was that it explained away the embarrassing inequality of the relation between nations—and races. Taking individual preferences and incomes as given, it was possible by means of a simple 'geometry of international trade' to show that 'world income' would be maximized under conditions of free exchange. The question of whether such a concept had any relevance or meaning, and of the severely restrictive conditions under which it might be applicable,[4] were usually disregarded when it came to policy recommendations.[5] In particular, the possibility that 'progress' might destroy traditional forms of social organization and endanger social and economic security for the many while benefiting the few was irrelevant as far as 'economics' was concerned; such upheavals could not be measured quantitatively in terms of goods and services. The fact that it was the capitalist who acquired the major part of the surplus arising from economic progress did not matter; his share was no more than the exact equivalent of his (marginal) contribution to that progress. That he happened to be British in the last century and American in this century, and that Britain then and America now have reaped the largest rewards from this progress, was regarded as a matter of luck or virtue: it was certainly not thought to alter the moral case.

There is no doubt that it was the leading country, Britain, and, subsequently, America (and after her recovery from World War II, within the Common Market, West Germany) which profited the most from this system. Moreover, as the strongest economic power in the nineteenth century, Britain had no need of government help or intervention, political ties or discriminatory privileges, in order more than to hold her own. On the contrary, by stripping government protection from industry in the non-self-governing colonies in the name of free trade, she condemned them to the status of mere appendages of her own industrial economic system. Since the colonial territories were poor, the development of their natural resources—at least in the context of this 'liberal' system—depended on their ability to supply international markets, especially Britain. Indeed, the mechanism enabled the metropolitan country to finance the required infrastructure investment through the monetization of these areas.[6] No conscious attempt was ever made to transform the economy of these areas with a view to raising output or incomes; but then nor was any conscious government intervention undertaken at home to buttress economic development. Since Britain was not only the most powerful market, but also the industrial pioneer, the growth of complementary economic systems in the dependencies was 'natural'. Any competitive pre-industrial manufactures existing in the colonies—such as Indian cotton—were destroyed. Non-discrimination palpably meant discrimination in favour of the strongest and most dynamic part of the system; this is clearly reflected in the cumulative problems with which the less developed areas have been faced as a result of the innovation and investment in the most powerful countries.[7]

No doubt this 'exploitation' was mainly unconscious; indeed it was automatic. A large supply of unskilled labour[8] depended on a closely controlled supply of capital from the metropolis. Foreign investment—apart from infrastructure—was, in the main, restricted to plantations and extractive industries. The infrastructure itself was mainly dependent on those enterprises. These investments—such as in banking or the railways—were manned by professional or skilled expatriate labour from the metropolitan country, receiving incomes substantially above those for similar jobs at home. This system was, perhaps, most thoroughly developed in the Belgian Congo (now Zaïre); only in South Africa was it carried further. In Algiers, even subordinate government jobs (such as postmen) were reserved mainly for the French. With the coming of liberation and the replacement of expatriates by the autochthonous population, class distinctions, severe inequality of income distribution and elitism were perpetuated. More recently the growing automation of production has enabled multi-national corporations to locate relatively labour-intensive processes in less developed areas. Since wages remain low and tax concessions are obtained, the bulk of the surplus again accrues to the dominant partner—the (mostly American) multi-national corporation which successfully plays off one small country against another. Interestingly enough, much the same sort of development characterizes the exploitation of North Sea oil and natural gas—only this time with Britain the loser.

Direct taxation was unknown and royalties were low. All this meant that an overwhelming part of the surplus flowed back to Britain, while wage rates for unskilled labour in the dependencies hardly rose at all. This dominant status was reinforced by an effective but informal preferential system —informal in the sense that it was not sanctioned by overt legislation. The managerial control of business in the dependencies was in British hands; with British tastes and technical experience, it was instinctive that Britain should have been the principal source of supplies. The picture was completed by the British character of the political administration; no deliberate planning was needed to round off this self-perpetuating system of supremacy.

However, protection and discrimination were needed for the establishment and growth of competitive industries in the United States, Germany and elsewhere in the middle of the nineteenth century. As a result, 'infant' industries in these countries had already overtaken Britain in a number of fields by the end of the century; Britain's supremacy had been eroded. *Mutatis mutandis* the picture applies after 1945: the Japanese, and even the German, 'miracle' was accomplished not by premature liberalization but by intensive investment.[9]

The astonishing feature of the post-war period has been that it was the United States which, flying in the face of conventional economic advice, acknowledged the failure of the war-time philosophy of 'freeish-trade *laissez-faire*'. Mainly as a result of the scare of Russian aggression, she organized large-scale aid for Europe and acquiesced in, indeed encouraged, discrimination against her own exports.[10] This was to last until the completion of Western European and Japanese reconstruction and the dramatic deterioration in her own balance of payments: this latter was not the result of 'high living' in the ordinary sense,[11] but rather the enormous weight of military expenditures abroad and of foreign investment.

The recovery of America's allies on the continent of Europe was promoted—and in Japan is still being promoted—by a policy of rigorous protection, now so comprehensibly and sharply resented by the United States. This resentment is hardly defensible when viewed in the neo-imperialist context of the ubiquitous expansion of large American multi-national firms on the basis of the increasing dollar balances of the 'host' countries; although it is perfectly justifiable in respect of the agricultural protectionism of Western Europe and of the industrial protectionism of Japan.

These experiences illustrate that there are cumulative forces at work which tend to inhibit or destroy harmonious co-existence between countries at different levels of development and with diverging dynamic and institutional characteristics. They have certainly destroyed the relevance of the neo-classical 'static model'.

In what follows we shall try to:

(i) restate the traditional doctrine of international trade, as applied in modern industrial conditions, from the viewpoint of power relationships;

(ii) suggest basic modifications, such as to explain actual developments;

(iii) review these issues in the light of historical economic experience and in the context of the post-war institutional framework; and

(iv) outline suggestions for an institutional and functional improvement of the international monetary system.

2. The Fancies Explored

1. DYNAMIC PROBLEMS AND STATIC MODELS

Economic theory accomplished the escape from the moral problems and conflicts of actual relations by means of a simple device—that is, by claiming universal and unconditional validity for a model of the economic system based on the assumption of perfect competition.[1] Atomistically organized producers, striving independently to maximize their own profits without regard for the actions of others, were assumed to supply identical, standard products to markets consisting of alert consumers in possession of all the facts, and with conscious, unalterable and independent tastes. This picture carried with it the implicit assumption of mutual independence as between demand and supply, and the postulation not only of perfect foresight, but the unchanging repetition of an identical process, in which accidental disturbances and their effects are smoothly eliminated and the original balance restored.

Functional relationships and behavioural assumptions were postulated not for their ability to elucidate what was happening in the real world, but because they yielded satisfying answers. The tendency to dismiss complications as perverse, without troubling to adduce evidence, became increasingly widespread. Definitional identities were used as if they were significant equations; relations between economic factors over limited periods culled from uncertain statistical material were assumed to be sufficiently stable and reversible to be used legitimately as bases for policy-making. In addition, it was assumed that these relationships were functionally independent of each other; for only then would it have been possible for the interaction of these relationships to yield unique and determinate equilibrium solutions.

Moreover, on the basis of data relating to different periods and often characterized by widely differing psychological conditions and institutional arrangements, it was allegedly possible to depict these hypothetical relationships by means of a collection of curves, each resembling the other in its mathematical (or at least diagrammatical) simplicity. In thus fitting curves to the various observed points, each curve, far from being a reflection of conditions in the real world, depicted formally a timelessly-enduring reversible relation between two variables—as (say) in the case of demand and supply curves. Any change was then analysed in terms of variations in the independent variable, all other factors being assumed constant. Hence, given the assumed mutual independence of supply and demand conditions and the existence of a timeless initial equilibrium position, any change in the initial configuration would produce a new repeatable equilibrium, its position being determined by the elasticities of the relevant schedules. But the comparison was between two *static* equilibria: nothing could be said about *how* the second position was to be reached or whether the system would return to the original 'equilibrium' if and when the 'disturbance' or alteration ceased.[2]

Even if the convenience of this *ceteris-paribus* method is conceded, one must have serious doubts as to its potential legitimacy—that is, as to whether such naively conceived relationships can ever be tested conclusively. Who can say whether any two observations are in fact situated on the same curve, in the sense that they conform to the postulated relationship? The difference of configuration might equally represent a movement *of* the curve, in other words reflect a modification of the assumed relationship, since the observations relate to different points in time. (If the collection of a number of observations stretches over a considerable time, it will inevitably increase the probability of the occurrence of far-reaching changes in the nature of the relationship putatively being observed, if indeed they can be said to exist at all). Such relationships, therefore, cannot be proven; equally, and of inestimable advantage to the 'scientists', they cannot be disproven. Their significance, as in the more obscure realms of abstract painting, is confined to the imagination of their creators.

If the existence of a schedule is inferred from a comparison of two historical observations, none the less it will serve only as a *description* of the change and not an *explanation*. Anything more would amount to implicit theorizing in the worst sense which, if used for predictive purposes, could be seriously misleading. Furthermore, if the schedule is not derived from historically observed changes, but rather is deduced from the original equilibrium on the basis of hypothetical considerations, neither the direction nor the magnitude of the shift can be predicted. It transpires that, if the 'final' equilibrium position is historically observable, the whole exercise is trivial; if it is not, then supply and demand cannot be assumed to be mutually independent. Further, the final equilibrium—which, in principle, need never (and in fact will never) be reached—cannot be legitimately derived from 'schedules' whose elasticities are assumed constant: changes as between the relevant variables are likely to be far from infinitesimal and this will have a significant impact on relative incomes. Not only this: it is impossible to predict such changes (in the relation between the variables) simply on the basis postulated by Marshall and other writers[3] since, even if we admit the existence of such schedules, the process of adjustment itself may, and probably will, alter their 'shape'. Hence, the position of the ultimate equilibrium will depend crucially on the antecedent historical circumstances and not merely on the values attaching to a single shift.[4]

If a two-country model constructed in this way evades several all-important problems, analysis in terms simply of two commodities obscures most others. The relation between the two commodities *defines* rather than explains the mechanism of change. The results obtained are trivial. If it is further assumed that these commodities cannot be 'inferior', that is, perverse reactions to price movements are excluded, a large area of the impact of innovation on trade is also eliminated from the scope of analysis, since the displacement of exports by innovation cannot be analysed in a two-country model. Problems of trade, especially international trade in manufactures, can hardly be investigated on these terms; far from being identical, goods change all the time. Thus price comparisons mean very little. It would, for this reason, be impossible to establish statistically with any accuracy whether the efficiency or the prices of a given country have risen relatively to another.

If the concept of 'goods' stands for aggregates, for 'bales' or baskets of products, index-number problems of the utmost difficulty arise, since any significant, non-infinitesimal, changes (such as need to be analysed) will distort the original comparative cost position, and change the composition of the aggregate. The consequences of this are highly pertinent. The Marshallian reciprocal demand curves in foreign trade, being *mixta composita*, obscure by their simplicity the extreme complexities underlying their 'shifts'—these being accompanied by, and inseparable from, changes in their shape. The concept of a shifted curve with an *ex-post* elasticity is even less legitimate.

Traditional theory, and particularly the traditional theory of international trade, was, as we have seen, founded on a strictly static model of the economic system, in which resources, including technical knowledge and tastes, were assumed to be given. There must have been in the mind of its propagators some idyllic picture of a tranquil (but most profitable) system of cost-minimization in which 'give factors of production' are capable of being reallocated *between* industries instantaneously and without any difficulty.[5] As long as this process in fact takes place in an environment of rustic simplicity—on *both* sides—such a picture might not have been a complete distortion. One could see Arcadian maidens turning from the milking of cows to the spinning of wool, without the risk that 'capital' would totally lose its value in the change. So long as 'resources' are taken to be land and (mobile) labour, with the attribute of easy adjustment between alternative uses, this view might have been acceptable: Jeffersonian agricultural America was perhaps the last instance of this blissful state. An easy reallocation would then be possible without the benefits of cheaper imports being offset by losses, the most painful of which would be the elimination of entrepreneurial ability.

But nothing could be further from modern reality than Arcadia. The problem now consists in the reciprocal influences (including trade between (generally speaking) unequal partners) which determine the rate and direction of growth of members of an open trading system. Trade will determine growth; and growth will determine trade. Capital accumulation, which raises the productivity of both land and labour; the advantages of large-scale production; technical progress: it is the pervasive importance of these three related factors which makes nonsense of the conventional approach.

It is easy to demonstrate, moreover, that in real life a few years' economic growth far outweighs in quantitative importance any conceivable 'improvement' resulting from a 'better allocation' of *given* resources, at any rate in 'rich' fully industrialized countries. The opening-up or liberalization of trade might lead to the underselling of the principal industries of weaker countries, so imparting a sharp deflationary shock to their economies, while the stronger countries who benefit thereby might in the process expand their own industries. The destruction of capital suffered by the poorer countries in this way might be irremediable. Trade between unequal partners is not likely to leave factor endowments unchanged; moreover, its impact will not be symmetrical (especially if the initial discrepancy is further widened as a result of biased technical progress).[6]

If the effects of accumulation and increasing returns are excluded by assumption from the traditional approach, so is the related problem of *technical progress* by postulating a 'given state' of technical knowledge. If at all, it is treated rather as an external, autonomous, once-for-all change to which there would be a slow adjustment in an otherwise completely change-less system. The model, conceived of in terms of unspecified countries, suggests a principle of symmetry whereby the impact of such a limited change is random or unbiased. No doubt it is admitted that some countries or areas *could* be hurt by change;[7] but the impression most insistently conveyed is that this would be the exception rather than the rule. No emphasis is laid on the continuity of the process and on its close connection with capital accumulation. Thus the consequential disturbance of the comparative advantage of the poorer areas, which have to rely for their exports on primary products produced by primitive methods, is disregarded.

The suggestion is that new technical knowledge would spread and thus increase incomes also outside the initiating focus of progress. This view neglects the basic difference between international trade among unequal partners and inter-regional trade within modern, highly integrated societies or Welfare States.[8] In a framework of disparate economic growth and in the absence of deliberate intervention by a sovereign agency, technical progress seems not merely to have increased disparities historically, but to have acted as a positive impediment to the development of the poorer areas.[9]

The competitive power of traditional (old-fashioned) producers is reduced by increases in technical knowledge and the consequential reduction in costs, and by the introduction of new and superior (or better-advertised) products, often more so even than as a result of the 'mere' accumulation of capital in the stronger countries.[10] Technical progress is, in these terms, likely to bring net benefits to the initiator of change—even though *some* of the victims of change are likely to be situated within its own political boundaries.[11]

The process will follow two continuous paths:

(i) refinements in the production of existing commodities and services, probably also produced by other countries; and

(ii) the discovery and development of new or radically improved products.

The former will enable luckier and more energetic producers to cut prices at home and abroad; the influence of the latter will be more far-reaching. It might lead to a displacement of older products and impose dangerously large price cuts or widespread structural changes on their suppliers. But if the new technique is radically different from the old (as in the case of the mechanical loom) then the displacement of existing suppliers as a result of developments under (i) above might be no less damaging or violent; prices might be forced down below levels capable of providing subsistence standards for workers in industries which did not benefit from the change.

In both cases it is probable that the technical improvement (embodied in new investment) will reduce the average labour requirement per unit of output. Labour will be relatively scarce or well organized in the dominant country and entrepreneurs will be under a strong incentive to exploit technical progress to relieve this scarcity. In the nature of things, therefore, research in the dominant country will tend to concentrate on technical problems, which, if solved, is bound to decrease the value of the productive factor relatively more abundant elsewhere. The fact that research expenditure tends to be concentrated cumulatively in the richest dynamic countries only intensifies this bias. The labour-saving propensities in a high-wage scarce-labour economy dominate the form of its inventions. The developed country will have achieved a quasi-monopoly position which allows not merely the displacement of the products of less developed countries, but provides the resources, through high quasi-rents, with which further to develop and justify its advantage.[12]

If parallel improvements in productivity do not occur in the poorer countries, where production is organized on a relatively land- or labour-intensive basis, their costs will be undercut by the dominant country and incomes will come under pressure. For example, the invention of artificial fibres or synthetic rubber has in each case reduced the relative price of the natural product; the improved process for the refinement of edible oil manufactures impoverishes olive-oil producers; the development of glass wool has depressed the market for cork. Most of the gain in these cases went to the manufacturer. Once the technical revolution has been accomplished there are a number of reasons why, in practice, it will become irreversible. Protectionism is only one such (if at times potent) reason. A subsequent reversal of the situation through the adoption abroad of the techniques of the dominant country might not much help foreign suppliers to regain lost markets in the dominant country (although it might help them in third countries). Once an industry has established itself it is unlikely to be allowed to disappear: asymmetry—as reflected in the 'kinked' curve—has to be accepted as the norm.

Indeed there is a danger that innovations might overshoot the mark,[13] thus threatening to weaken the poorer areas even further. In such cases the former comparative disadvantage of the dominant country in the production of hitherto labour-intensive products will disappear. Once this happens, superior marketing techniques and other institutional factors may even result in that industry being transformed into an exporter. Not only industry, but also agriculture, may be so affected, as in the case of rice in the United States. The devastating effects of the rise of the British textiles industry on India is a good example. Apart from Hong Kong, Taiwan and South Korea (and the southern United States) there is hardly a case where 'cheap labour', without initial protection, led to the rise of competitive industry.

The historical neglect of *decreasing costs* in the traditional theory can also be seen to have been inexcusable. Far from being the rare exception, economies of scale have embraced an ever-widening field—not excluding a considerable part of agriculture. Once the importance of increasing returns is admitted, however, and their nature analysed, they can be seen to be largely irreversible; in other words the historically observable relationship between output and capital is unique, in the sense of being reciprocally connected with the conjunction of capital accumulation and technical progress. On the one hand, in poor areas the difficulties and imperfections of effective decision-making and the lack of entrepreneurial ability and capital vitiate the assumption that potential fields of investment opened up by trade will be automatically exploited.[14] The 'exceptional' case of infant industries expands to encompass infant *countries* and *regions*, and discriminatory policies become essential to any sane conception of maximum economic progress.

On the other hand, in the rich, progressive areas, there loom the so-called pecuniary external economies—windfall profits which can be reaped by nearly all as growth accelerates. In a rapidly growing economy, the risk of mis-investment diminishes, and an increasing number benefit from the intensification of activity. The faster the rate of accumulation the more are conclusions arrived at on the basis of constant factor endowments (and costs) likely to become nugatory and misleading.

The possibility of recurrent obsolescence and unemployment without any compensating advantages will necessarily increase the riskiness of enterprise in the weak countries.[15] The incentive to invest will then be further reduced, an effect which is distinct from, but additional to, the equally un-favourable deflationary pressure imposed by the greater flexibility of the more dynamic economies upon the poor and weak; this last will arise on the one hand through the non-price advantage of quick deliveries—which can only be secured at the cost of under-employment in less dynamic economies—and on the other hand through credit facilities. It is obvious also from experience that money-wages do not in modern conditions necessarily rise in proportion with increases in productivity; this means that the money-cost per unit of output in a rapidly growing economy will tend to rise more slowly than in sluggish economies, even if the slow growth in real income does not create dissatisfaction and lead to cost-inflationary pressures.

2. INTERNATIONAL ECONOMIC RELATIONS AS A PROBLEM OF OLIGOPOLY

The importance of the 'short-run' path of readjustment can hardly be exaggerated: it will determine the outcome of the balancing process which, if the initial imbalance has been considerable, will be historically almost certainly unique. The segregation of the 'long-run' or 'real' factor-alloca-tion problem from 'short-run' or 'monetary' phenomena can only produce nonsensical results. It can be said that most, if not all, of the important economic relationships (that is, between countries) have been completely eliminated in the classical and neo-classical approach to the problem. This was partly achieved by relying, so far as monetary affairs were concerned, on the assumption of a bullion standard—or a standard so closely linked to gold as to make no difference, for example the Peelite ideal of the British currency system—while the bulk of the micro-argument was conducted in terms of 'real' values, whether classical labour values or neo-classical opportunity costs. In this way was the atomistic character of international trade asserted, to which could be applied the rules of perfect competition; thus, the relationship between members of different trading countries could be subsumed under a general-equilibrium system. Such an approach entirely ignored, on the one hand, the changing structure of the world economy (in particular the impact of new monetary Institutions) and, on the other, the undiminished (if not increasing) inequality between countries.

This approach derived, of course, from the classical non-monetary two-country–two-commodity model of international trade, in which one of the countries was assumed to be infinitely larger than the other, hence represent-ing 'the rest of the world'. In brief, countries were in turn expected to operate on a perfectly (or atomistically) competitive basis, the implications of which were that the policies or aggregate actions of any one country had no noticeable effects on the situation, objectives or policies of any other. By construing the balance of payments as principally a matter concerning specie flows initiated by individuals, which in turn led to further expenditure decisions, in the two-country context, the whole problem of dynamic adjustment was avoided.

The mechanism by which equilibrium is allegedly regained after some disturbance is formulated either in terms of elasticities, or in terms of book-keeping identities, such as savings and investment; hence the effects of devaluation or the payment of reparations can be analysed on the basis of partial schedules, depicting the relationship between the demand for exports and imports and their price. Alternatively, change can be analysed in the context of simple Keynesian relations such as the marginal propensity to import or the margin of unused capacity. In neither system are the functional relationships or propensities altered as a result of the disturbance and of the adjustment to it.

Foreign trade itself leads to specialization, and it is only in the most trivial of cases that the assumption of perfectly competitive behaviour between individuals in different countries and between countries themselves can be considered meaningful or plausible. The interposition between productive units of the monetary, fiscal and commercial policies of States of vastly differing size, moreover, adds a further element in international trade relations which conflicts with the assumption of perfect competition. This would be the case even if perfect competition prevailed on the level of the individual or the firm, which, patently, it does not.

Suppose, for instance, we wished (with Marshall) to determine 'how far the terms of trade and the volume of trade would be changed if, trade between two countries E and G having been in equilibrium, there is a considerable increase in E's demand for G's goods unaccompanied by any corresponding increase of demand on the part of G'.[16] The first effect would be a change in the balance of trade (and this cannot be assumed away by uttering magical incantations about long-run positions, as it must be repeated over and over again, because the locus of the 'long-run equilibrium', if such a concept is at all meaningful, will be co-determined by what happens as a result of the disturbance in the balance of trade). This will affect the balance of trade of the trading partner, not only directly, but also through (though separately from) the price change. What will happen next is in the lap of the gods. The emergence of the imbalance might or might not be followed by retaliatory measures in the other country (countries), which will have the effect of offsetting and frustrating the direct consequences of the initial impulse. Cumulative movements will then ensue. Total demand, that is demand in both (all) countries taken together, might start to fall or rise and the balance of trade might become the object of an oligopolistic struggle. To attempt to analyse these effects on the basis of diagrams purporting to set out the final equilibrium position without enquiring whether (and how) the intermediate stages leading to that position are at all

feasible is to prejudge the outcome of the exercise. The path of the adjustment through time, the impact of the psychological atmosphere (particularly where conscious bluff is concerned) on that path and, hence, on
the ultimate outcome of the adjustment are not a matter of indifference.

Edgeworth's treatment of Marshall's 'static' geometry of reciprocal
demand curves implicitly recognized this, although he failed to realize the
decisive importance of the consequential limitation. He compared reciprocal
supply–demand curves to the hands of a clock, which are activated by a
mechanism behind its face. 'A movement along a supply-and-demand curve
of international trade should be considered as attended with rearrangements
of internal trade; as the movement of the hand of a clock corresponds to
considerable unseen movements of the machinery.'[17] This analogy brings
out clearly that both Marshall and Edgeworth thought of the relation
between an initial causal change and the resulting new 'equilibrium' as
something given and enduring. The clock can only go at a predetermined
pace and move the hands in a predetermined way.

The relationship between the initial change in the balance of payments
and consequential developments is, of course, of an entirely different and
more attenuated nature: it will also depend on the historical position and,
in turn, determine anticipations, that is, the reactions of the countries, producers, etc., involved. This fact is of decisive importance. If the mechanism
resembles that of a clock at all, it is a very peculiar one: the movements of
the hand necessarily influence the working of the 'machinery', and it is
equally possible that 'off-scene' happenings will have varying effects on the
movement of the hands with changes in the conjecture or in psychological
climate. The *ex-ante* schedule and its elasticity are not necessarily relevant
since they are highly likely to change with developments through time; in
any case, it is thoroughly illegitimate to assume *a priori* that they are
constant. The *ex-post* schedule, on the other hand, depends on the historical
sequence of events (e.g. their impact on the level and urgency of demand
in each country), on the impact of these on anticipations, all of which will
influence accumulation and, hence, the country's competitive strength. If
there exists a causal relationship between the initial change and these
subsequent autonomous impulses, these latter can no longer be ignored as
being of a second order of importance. The assumption that we are confronted with reversible relationships and that, therefore, the comparison
of final equilibrium positions can yield meaningful answers for predictive
purposes is fallacious.

If the path from the original position is not uniquely determined, and if a
number of final equilibria were possible, depending on what happened as
a result of the first autonomous impulse or change (including consequential
policies adopted), then the comparative analysis of two given final equilibrium situations will not yield *generally* acceptable conclusions. Long-run
equilibrium will, in fact, never be established, because the whole system

will be undergoing continual change, the adjustments to the 'first' disturbance never being permitted fully to work themselves out.

Nor are resources 'given' in the long run. Not only does accumulation take place all the time, but trade has been, and necessarily will be, one of the main determinants of the growth of resources, especially those vital resources, capital, entrepreneurial ability and technical skill. Relative factor endowments and comparative costs are, therefore, continually changing as a direct result of the very trade to which their divergences as between countries allegedly (viz. Heckscher–Ohlin) give rise. Consequently the eventual outcome, the precise character and shape of any so-called equilibrium position reached after adjustment, is analytically inseparable from the path of that adjustment.[18]

At the simplest level, and in the context of a *given* framework of policy and conjuncture, one may say that the imports and exports of a country will be determined by:

(i) the relation of money-costs and incomes at home and abroad at existing exchange rates;

(ii) the relation of prices of goods and services entering into international trade at home and abroad;

(iii) the relation of demand to productive capacity at home and abroad which, in turn, will be influenced at the margin by the rate of investment; and

(iv) anticipations about the stability of these relationships.

However, these factors will be far from independent of each other. Changes in the terms of trade, for instance, will affect incomes, and all changes in incomes will affect prices and, possibly, the sensitivity of demand to changes in price. Moreover, changes in price resulting from autonomous increases in costs will have effects totally different from those due to changes in demand. This aspect of the problem, vitally important under modern conditions, is, of course, ruled out *a priori* by the assumption of perfect (atomistic) competition in the market for goods and services both in domestic and international trade.

There is, further, a twilight zone in which increases in money incomes will have disproportionate effects, irrespective of the price changes that may occur. As full employment is approached, domestic supply comes under pressure. Imports rise. The sensitivity of demand to increases in foreign prices decreases. Thus, the development of productive capacity and the dynamism of the economy (which determine the point at which shortages arise) will play a decisive part in determining the balance of payments. If the traditional Quantity Theory is irrelevant because it cannot account for the effects of increases in productive capacity, the primitive Keynesian 'absorption' approach is no more sophisticated.

Analysis must, therefore, take into account the comparative relation between income and capacity in each country. This, however, gives rise to the possibility that secondary effects may assume a greater importance than primary changes, with the former, in the longer run, offsetting or more than offsetting the latter. It is this factor, moreover, which introduces perhaps the most hated element into this crucial part of basic economic theory—indeterminacy—for, as a result, generalizations become precarious, if not illicit.

It should also be noted that relative incomes at home and abroad are inextricably related with prices. Equally, the interaction between prices, incomes and demand will differ according to the historical configuration of a particular situation: this because international trade and the money economy makes prices depend not only on wants, but also on price expectations. All these factors will be decisively influenced by (a) the structure of both sides of industry and their relations with each other and with the government, and (b) their historical experience, both of which follow from the basically oligopolistic nature of the product market and the bilaterally monopolistic character of the labour market. Thus, with stability co-determined by historical antecedents, a second, fundamental and multiple kind of indeterminacy pervades the system.

Equilibrium theory postulates that if all individuals take the right decision in some sense, equilibrium and optimum conditions will prevail. This presupposes that there exists some independently given and determinate set of right decisions. But there is no such set. What will happen depends on what people do now—and what people do now depends on what has happened in the past and how they interpret the present and view the future. Where prices are determined by price-expectations—and the latter might justify concessions to pressures on costs (wages or dividends), which in turn justify the price-expectations—the optimum is not only clouded in ignorance of the future, but it is indeterminate. Finally, as we have seen, all this is related to accumulation and technical progress, which are also historically determined.

We have seen in the foregoing how the traditional approach to international relations, by confining itself to the sterile analysis of trade between (usually two) anonymous countries, has produced a body of theory which is at worst positively misleading, and at best merely vacuous. In particular, by ignoring the crucial intermediary position of States in the international relations of 'productive units' or other economic agents, the analysis has become characterized by a sort of monetary perfect competition, so that the reactions of these units to the policies of others can be disregarded. In fact, international monetary affairs are dominated by oligopoly between States (and, more recently, among multi-national corporations) and by the sort of oligopolistic struggle that this may entail. Differences in size (in terms of national income, investment and trade) and power of resistance (in terms of relative holdings of liquid international reserves) of countries are decisive factors in the final outcome of any imbalance, however caused. Moreover,

the absolute size of any payments imbalance will have different consequences for employment, economic growth (in so far as productivity and
savings are affected), incomes and prices in any given country, depending on
its size, dependence on foreign trade and psychological sensitivity. Furthermore, the size of a country's reserves will have a decisive influence in this
respect, since it is only reserves—including short-term credits if held in
sufficient quantities[19]—that can guarantee it freedom from foreign interference and from having to give in to bluffs.[20] The disregard of these
problems is the more serious because anticipations of a repetition of
trouble might precipitate further trouble, thereby excluding certain types
of policy (for instance, depreciation or exchange-rate flexibility) because of
the risk of destructive hedging speculation.[21]

As soon as the assumption of perfect competition is dropped, therefore,
and the fatuity of Say's law recognized, our view of, and method of analysing, the relation between individual and State, and relations within each
category, necessarily change. What Professor Haberler, in his restatement
of the free-trade case, called 'monopolistic doctoring of the terms of trade'
refers not to actions taken by individuals on an assessment of their own
market power, but to measures taken by the government which impinge
on all or most individuals within given national boundaries—even if not
in an identical manner—and thus take on the aspect of collective action.

I have dealt with the problem of the limitation of the free-trade case
elsewhere.[22] Here I shall confine myself strictly to the problems connected
with the purposive management by countries of their balance of payments.

The assumption that international trade is conducted by individual
firms, with the role of the monetary mechanism being restricted to the
automatic transmission of impulses from the 'real' side, depends, as we have
seen, on the acceptance of a rigid set of rules governing that mechanism.
This was, perhaps, an accurate picture in respect of the primitive gold
standard.[23] So long as the central banks were 'politically' independent, and
merely registered gains and losses of gold, the Humean mechanism could
still be thought to some extent effective. It was already being increasingly
modified by differences in the 'efficiency' in the use of gold, in the rate of
growth of international liquidity (gold and, formerly, silver), and in the
rate of growth of capital (which was considerably influenced by it). This
phase of development had ended already before 1914 in Western Europe—
and elsewhere even earlier. Since World War II, the theoretical framework
has been completely at variance with reality; any conclusions based upon
it will, therefore, be highly unreliable.[24]

As soon as it is recognized that the first impact of changes in international
trading will affect *countries*—through their balance of payments—and that
it is *countries* that will react, the problem appears in a new light. If the
relationship of individual producers in highly developed areas cannot be
analysed in terms of perfect (atomistic) competition, how much less is such

an analysis applicable to relations between a very restricted number of countries, each of whom is exporting a more or less limited range of products of which it is an important supplier?[25]

The character of the adjustment process will be seen to be determined by the impact of the balance of trade deficit (or surplus) and the consequential income changes and policy decisions on the country's foreign balance. In this particular case, it would be necessary to know (as we have indicated) the size of the country in relation to its trading partners, the fraction of its trade with each country in the trading system, its employment and price conjuncture, its gold and currency reserve positions, *and, in addition*, within these external limitations, its *capacity* to implement any policy from a range of *available* and *feasible* alternative policy weapons (for instance, the extent of its machinery for imposing direct controls or taxes).[26] All these factors will determine—should the policies of the member countries of the trading system differ—which countries are in a position to bluff their way out of trouble and which will have to give in if bluffed because (say) of a shortage of reserves or of their inability to influence the incomes of their trading partners. Such factors will also determine which countries will dominate in the sphere of economic development and which will be dominated.[27]

It can be seen, therefore, that such propositions as 'devaluation will improve the balance of trade if the sum of the elasticities is such and such' are either trivial or meaningless.[28] For we must know the reaction of world income and demand to the measures proposed, and their relation to world productive capacity (itself one of the determinants—and at the same time not independent—of the measures), to know what will happen. In a 'world' near to full employment, 'elasticities' might be 'perverse',[29] in other words, price increases in any one country will not necessarily reduce (or prevent an increase in) its exports.[30] Changes in income both shift and alter the shape of the 'schedules' which traditional analysis assumes to be 'given'; the 'elasticity-mongers' take as constant those things which must necessarily change. In fact, 'world' demand for imports is not unequivocally determined by 'real' factors, and its price-elasticity is subject to violent fluctuations due to variations in the level of employment. Nor does it necessarily improve with the passage of time. In periods of intense oligopolistic struggle for international reserves, it may even worsen, even so far as single countries are concerned.[31] What happens, as we have demonstrated, will depend on the (historical) monetary relation between income and productive capacity and the anticipations attaching to each of these factors. The policy of each country, in its turn, will be influenced by the condition of its balance of payments and reserves, and, in framing it, few countries—with the possible exception of the United States—will be able to disregard the policy of others in the rest of the trading system.[32] Perfect monetary competition is a figment.

Once full employment is approached, 'flexibility' in a single country diminishes, unless there is rapid growth. Yet if full employment is not maintained growth will slow down and the country will suffer in the long run from a relative eclipse in innovations and investment—for instance, in the United States since 1953, and in Britain wellnigh since 1880. Devaluation, which has been advocated as a means of achieving full employment without the need for international agreement, turns out to be a broken reed. Not only might its 'effectiveness' be wrecked by repetition through the creation of a new pattern of expectations, but its effects on a fully employed economy are self-defeating, since they engender inflationary pressures which increase home demand and imports. These are difficult to resist, even on the first occasion, and almost impossible to resist on repetition.

We may enumerate, then, certain decisive factors, apart from those automatic price- and income-effects which impinge on the domestic economy, which will determine the deliberate reaction of a government to, say, a deficit in its balance of payments, given the degree of freedom with which it can operate and implement those policies:

(i) the *principles of policy*, that is, whether the government, for example, wants (a) to stabilize employment, (b) to maintain reserves, or (c) to maintain price-stability;

(ii) the *latitude of choice politically open as between policy instruments with which to carry out policy*, for example, whether restricted to 'global' monetary controls or capable of implementing direct controls;

(iii) the *degree to which the country depends on foreign trade*, since substantial dependence might make compensatory policies difficult, if not impossible;

(iv) the *availability of international reserves*, and their size relative to the country's imports and payments obligations; and

(v) the country's *relative economic power*, measured by its share in world industrial output and ownership of natural resources.

Generalizations will always be difficult; yet it might reasonably be suggested that if the majority of countries—or at least those most powerful and economically independent—were bent on policies (i) (b) or (c), their primary aim *not* being the maintenance of employment, then a deflationary bias is likely to be imparted to the world system as a whole. Generally speaking, it is easier to enforce deflation than to stabilize employment. *The risk of a total loss of reserves during a crisis before the world situation changes is obvious and immediate. There are no obvious and immediate financial risks incurred by tolerating unemployment or by promoting an increase in reserves.* The risk consists in foregoing growth. But this becomes apparent in the long run only, and responsibility for it can be explained away unless unemployment rises to politically intolerable levels. These levels will be judged differently from country to country and the degree of tolerance will depend to a considerable extent on historical experience. If a runaway inflation has devastated an unprepared community, its desire to guard against rapidly rising prices will be the more acute. The behaviour of continental countries demonstrates this tendency clearly. Their anti-inflationary sensitivity is far higher than Britain's, for example, despite the fact that in their historical experience unemployment, if it has not been as persistent, has been almost as serious as in the Anglo-Saxon countries, whose traumatic experience and dominant motive fear is mass unemployment.

The problem of holding balance is not easy. It takes deliberate initiative to counteract a gain in reserves by increasing demand when the world as a whole is suffering from deflation, that is from a general deficiency of demand. Inaction will probably lead to yet further gains in reserves. Hence, in an oligopolistic struggle or 'game' situation the ultimate retreat will almost certainly be towards maximizing reserves or minimizing gold losses. The convention which speaks of the 'strength' of currencies and the need for 'conserving' reserves, and which greets favourably the inflow of gold while labelling the exchange of non-income-bearing gold for high-income-bearing assets as a 'crisis', will tend to strengthen this bias. It could be overcome, but probably only with international agreement.[33]

An obverse aspect of this problem is the tendency for countries who do not boast of having and cherishing reserve currencies to indulge in a de-valuation bias. This has been the cause of increasingly shrill complaints on the part of the United States and its sharply 'nationalistic' turn in policy.[34] I shall try to demonstrate that such a devaluation bias is unfeasible if the country suffers from a disproportionate tendency to cost-inflation, because that tendency would be further accelerated, in which event the devaluation would lose its bite.

The conclusion suggested by these considerations is of the vital impor-tance, on the one hand, of preventing the spread of deflation as a result of shortages (or anticipated shortages) in reserves and, on the other, of ensur-ing that any increased facility to create international reserves would not be abused, in the sense of it sustaining the inflationary spiral in certain coun-tries which, in the end, would permeate the rest of the world trading sys-tem. Thus, there is a pressing need for a strong central organ with the responsibility of guaranteeing the feasibility of creating sufficient inter-national reserves to obviate such cumulative deflation. The severe crises experienced by the United States prior to the establishment of the Federal Reserve System—themselves the result of the very absence of such an insti-tution—seems sufficient evidence to carry this point. The value of—and the need for—the accumulation of reserves by any country is immediately re-duced when their creation is provided for by some central authority. At the same time, this should diminish cut-throat competition for their ownership, thereby relieving pressure on the world economy and dramatically decreas-ing the risk of a general liquidation of credit. On the other hand, access to such a central organ would have to be regulated. Agreed rules of conduct would have to be established. Unfortunately the events of the last few years do not suggest that such a balanced approach to one of the most important international economic problems has yet found acceptance. There is a continued yearning for the extremes of ancient orthodoxy, for a return to the fallacies of the past, whereby 'perfect competition' would be rediscovered by the application of legal sanctions against 'monopolies'—especially trade unions[35]—and the convertibility (if not merging) of currencies restored. We shall have to deal with these problems in greater detail in the historical part of this essay.

3. A THEORY OF RESERVE-HOLDING[36]

(a) *The need for international reserves*

The desirable level of any country's reserves,[37] as we have seen, cannot be determined without reference to its policy aims, nor without regard to whatever conventional restrictions may be impinging on its choice of policy instruments as a means to readjustment. Moreover, any disparity of policy aims as between countries, or the outlawing of certain direct (and therefore quick-acting) measures to restore balance, will in this framework necessitate a countervailing increase in available reserves or in the powers of reserve creation. Claims that there exists a close relationship between the volume of international trade and the need for reserves, or between the level of reserves and the velocity of international monetary circulation, the level of demand and, hence, prices and the balance of payments, represent an unfortunate retrogression to darker ages initiated by Professor Friedman and taken up with such relish by the International Monetary Fund.[38, 39]

A most important influence affecting the sensible level of a country's international reserves, apart from its own policies and the political framework in which they are pursued, will be the prevailing policy climate in other, *leading*, countries. That is to say, the adequacy of a country's reserves will depend on the success—not to say willingness and capacity—with which the dominant members of an open trading system can avoid demand- and, even more dangerous, cost-inflation, by means other than indirect fiscal or monetary restriction. Otherwise the opposite calamity of deflation (or cyclical fluctuations between the two) could not be avoided. It will also depend on whether the dominant countries are prepared to maintain a position of full employment for long periods while limiting their current-account surpluses to levels that correspond to the rate of capital transfer to less advanced (though including industrialized) trading partners.

The need for liquidity is a combined function of the size of likely imbalances, that is, of the volume of international payments, and the magnitude and duration of their disequilibrium. Fundamentally, this is determined by the policy framework—in particular the range of 'admissible' means of readjustment—and the ends of policy. Especially important in this respect is the degree of unemployment and deceleration of growth that countries will tolerate before resorting to beggar-my-neighbour policies.

It should be noted, further, that a very large proportion of total trade and payments is concentrated among a few major powers. The number of these effectively independent units is further reduced by regional groupings, based on key banking centres and key currencies and sometimes, as in the case of the Sterling Area until the introduction of convertibility, backed by explicit institutional arrangements.[40] The more complementary a regional grouping, the freer it is in the choice of means—or the less intent it is to achieve policy aims not shared by the rest of the world—and the smaller its need for reserves.[41] Shared policy goals, whatever their nature, whether the avoidance of unemployment or of reserve losses, will in any case reduce this need (for reserves) for the world as a whole. Thus the conventional assumption that the pursuit of 'sound' policies all round will reduce the need for reserves is accurate; it amounts to the basic principle that countries cannot attempt to maintain employment and exchange rates if some powerful ones refuse to do so.[42]

If, on the other hand, the maintenance of employment is a universally declared policy, and governments are willing and able to intervene promptly in the event of inflationary or deflationary shocks by all appropriate means—including direct controls and incomes policy—the minimum safe levels of reserves will be far smaller than in a system in which prolonged unemployment is tolerated—or even induced to secure price-stability—in dominant countries, while others try to avoid competitive deflationary policies. A system which freely permits capital movements, even those of a speculative nature, will, under modern conditions, require far higher reserves than a system in which speculative flows are severely discouraged.[43] It is the volume and instability of *payments*, not merely of *current trade*, which is the rational determinant of reserve requirements.

A country that attempts to maintain employment without adequate means aimed at avoiding excessive inflation[44] will find its currency coming under increasingly heavy pressure. If such a country is weak or small there will follow either a currency crisis (associated with a fall in its external value) or a discontinuation of the policy of full employment. If, however, the country concerned is the centre of a large international currency system (as it has been lately), its trading partners might be induced to continue accumulating its currency for fear of the consequences of its depreciation (if they refuse). *Effective* convertibility into a reserve medium over which the key-currency country has no command would bring about such depreciation, but not without potentially awkward deflationary pressures or competitive exchange depreciations all round.

We have seen that the relationship of the member countries of the world economy with each other is in effect one of oligopoly; countries will trim their behaviour according to that of others. The discouraging feature of this state of affairs is that, as long as international reserves are scarce (or thought to be scarce), behaviour that tends to induce gains in reserves will be at a premium, since severe losses of reserves must induce others to follow suit in such policies. Thus, a scarcity of reserves is likely to aggravate itself, while uncertainty about the monetary strategy of strong countries would have the same result. Since 'safety first' would counsel deflation, international monetary reform must aim at eliminating this most insidious long-term danger.

There is a further reason why it is only too likely that the system should have a bias against growth and full employment and in favour of the avoidance of reserve losses, at whatever cost in terms of expansion. Under modern conditions, adherence to the 'classic' rules, demanding symmetrical expansion and contraction, might seem incompatible with domestic stability[45]—especially price-stability.[46] If the problem of domestic inflation cannot be solved by policies which do not impinge on the balance of payments (by their effect on employment), a balanced functioning of the world payments system will not prove possible. Any increase in reserves will then represent a deflationary impact abroad, because it originates in a cut in demand.[47]

(b) *The cost–benefit of international reserves*

The acquisition of international reserves by any one country as a result of export surpluses or of borrowing—instead of using them to pay for imports—represents a real sacrifice in terms of investment or consumption foregone. This sacrifice can be justified only if it enables the holding country to increase its rate of economic growth and investment over time— in the case of disturbances in its balance of international payments—in excess of what would have been possible without such reserves. Inasmuch as the initial level of investment would have been higher had the export surplus not been used to accumulate reserves, this means that the reserves, in order to be economically justifiable, must serve as a protection to the economy, so much so as to enable it to grow at least as fast on the average— because free from the deflationary implications of periodic balance-of-payments disturbances—as it would have had those reserves not been accumulated, but used for productive investment instead. These disturbances can originate either abroad, that is, in a fall in demand for exports (or a flight of capital), or internally, for example through a crop failure. 'Free' reserves are, therefore, one of the means by which the need for interrupting the growth of the economy may be obviated and steady growth over time secured.[48] Only by fulfilling this role can the sacrifice incurred by keeping resources uninvested be justified. But the use of reserves for investment is a one-for-all gain; only if the consequential increase in national income results in a further increase in investment would it have continuing cumulative beneficial effects.

The forgoing of increased investment implied by a cumulative increase in reserves, then, reduces the potential maximum rate of growth. But, if an increase in the rate of growth enhances the possibility of accelerating the growth of income without imperilling the balance of payments—and eventually enables the country to acquire reserves without slowing down growth —the accumulation of reserves is not justified. It should be noted that policy measures—for instance, exchange or import controls—which obviate cuts in investment in the event of balance-of-payments difficulties would reduce the need for reserves.

The other alternative is borrowing. The choice between borrowing and reserve-holding will depend on the terms on which the former can be procured,[49] compared with the loss of real income as a result of holding reserves (which might themselves yield some income). We might conclude then:

(i) the poorer the country and the smaller its supply of capital, the greater, probably, will be the sacrifice entailed by holding reserves in terms of potential income forgone;

(ii) the sacrifice on the part of the poorer countries might be reduced if they kept their reserves in the form of freely marketable, income-earning assets,[50] although the maximum rate of income earned in this way must be well below the increase in domestic output and income forgone;

(iii) poorer countries will probably have greater need for holding reserves than richer ones, for two reasons. First, there is the notorious instability of primary-product markets and harvests, on which such countries mostly rely, hence increasing the vulnerability of their balance of payments; second, the ability of poorer countries to obtain credits on reasonable terms is much less than that of rich countries in the absence of purposive international arrangements;

(iv) limitations on the choice of policy instruments, for example the prohibition of direct controls over imports and exports, impose disproportionate burdens on poorer countries. Their acceptance of such burdens is rational only if international arrangements are effective in offsetting them by means of special grants or credit facilities;

(v) the sacrifice of investment and income as a result of accumulating reserves must none the less be weighed (as we have noted) against the increased capacity that this will afford in withstanding sudden emergencies which would otherwise involve sharp deflationary action and consequent loss of income.

If reserves are held in the form of the assets of another country, this will have the effect of increasing international liquidity, since the accumulation of exchange is the alternative to acquiring gold. This introduces a further complication, because the acquisition of these key-currency assets instead of gold has a relatively inflationary impact. If the former happened in a situation of all-round full employment, and if the financial centre disregarded in its policy-making the increase in its liabilities, the process might facilitate general inflation. This danger has been much emphasized. The expansion of the sterling standard after World War I and the building-up of the dollar-exchange standard after World War II, through which the United States was gradually freed from any regard for its balance-of-payments deficits, are as good examples as any. 'Losses' of reserves were nullified by other countries holding increasing dollar balances which they must have increasingly realized to be *de facto* inconvertible.[51]

If the build-up of a gold-exchange standard might encourage undue expansion, the liquidation of such a system represents an even greater risk and one to which less attention has been paid.[52] Yet this has happened at almost regular biennial intervals in the case of Britain and contributed much to the severity of the balance-of-payments crises which have constituted such an obstacle to British economic expansion. The Americans, alone, perhaps, are able to disregard such a deterioration in their overall international payments position.

3. The Facts Restated

1. OLIGOPOLY IN PRACTICE: THE RETREAT FROM BRETTON WOODS

(a) Bretton Woods and after

Towards the end of World War II a number of economists, oppressed by the overwhelming problem of unemployment between the wars (though it had disappeared during the first), were anxious to extend decisively the scope of monetary and economic co-operation. A start had already been made in this direction by the principal central banks of the world. They had even established an institution to this end just before the crisis of 1931 in the form of the Bank for International Settlements. That institution, however, proved to be singularly ineffective when, in the wake of the Crash and subsequent Depression, a general enforced liquidation and self-intensifying loss of confidence led ultimately to an almost total monetary collapse. The B.I.S. had been unable to avert catastrophe because it had been unable to organize the effective extension of the well-established principle of lender of last resort to international affairs; and both the B.I.S. and the Financial and Economic Committee of the League of Nations were unable (mainly as a consequence of French resistance) effectively to coordinate measures, if not to sustain demand, then at least to prevent it from shrinking further.[1]

Subsequently the B.I.S. was to incur political odium on account of its alleged collaboration with the Nazi régime immediately before and during World War II. Finally (yet perhaps most important) wartime experience had pointed to the need for governments rather than central bankers to be in control, if an international institution designed to assist in the maintenance of external balance and internal stability was to operate satisfactorily.

External balance was seen as one of the conditions of attaining full employment while preserving internal stability. The uneven boom of the 1920s, the undermining of stability through the expedients of competitive exchange-rate depreciation and undervaluation, culminating in the disaster of the 1930s and war, were still vividly in mind. The preambles of all international economic pronouncements and agreements paid obeisance to the need for avoiding a repetition of that experience, even on a minor scale.[2]

The history of international monetary arrangements since the war has nevertheless been a chequered one. On the one hand stand great achievements. Employment has been maintained, in sharp contrast to the inter-war period as a whole. Material progress has been secured on an unprecedented scale, both in the highly developed and in the poor countries. Even in countries which grew more slowly than the average, such as the United States and Britain, the rate of expansion has nevertheless been far higher than before the war. (The relative decline of Britain had been masked before the war, however, by the ability to mobilize large parts of the world—even beyond its own vast empire—for the maintenance of its people's prosperity.) Technical and resource aid to the less developed countries has been made available on a scale never before equalled. Judged against the fears of a return to inter-war misery, the performance has been remarkable.

Yet so far as international monetary agreements are concerned, it has been a case of 'too little, too late'. The wartime reforms in the international monetary system at Bretton Woods can hardly claim much credit for such achievements as there were. The arrangements worked out between 1943 and 1945 broke down as early as 1947. Neither the means made available, nor the rules of the game—and therefore the choice of policy weapons at hand—proved adequate for the reconstruction of a war-shattered world economy.

The potential creditor countries, then under the leadership of the United States, followed closely if, quixotically, by the United Kingdom, took a rather *laissez-faire* restrictionist view. More accurately, this amounted to a stand against direct controls and in favour of indirect, fiscal and monetary, controls—this because they feared themselves, and therefore their potential export surpluses, to be vulnerable to waves of imported inflation from deficit countries who, rather than succumb to the 'discipline' of enforced deflation and unemployment, would seek instead to impose direct controls. As a result, both devaluation and direct controls were to be made difficult, if not impossible, without the consent of the United States. Debtor countries in their turn foresaw that, in the event of a slump, they would have to shoulder the whole burden of adjustment. They were anxious, therefore, to ensure that means would be provided whereby recalcitrance on the part of persistent creditors could be overcome by international action. They had no luck. What emerged was a compromise that favoured the potential creditor standpoint, in other words, that of the United States. Instead of Keynes's Clearing Union, itself less than a world central bank, there appeared the International Monetary Fund.

My opposition to the pre-Bretton Woods proposals as they emerged from the Anglo-American negotiations, and to the Final Act, was based on a belief that they were an attempt to enforce rules that embodied the jejune, if not more sinister,[3] notion that the war-torn world economy could be reconstructed and subsequently regulated according to the principles of a theoretical model characterized by perfect competition and constant or decreasing returns to scale in production.[4] It was assumed, in other words, that the countries of the world were united by a harmony of interests and that world income (whatever that may mean) could in some sense be optimized by making trade and payments as free as possible and by restoring currency convertibility at an early date, irrespective of the policies that creditor countries might be pursuing.

I have always thought this view to be hopelessly wrong-headed. The true character of the world economy is far removed from this picture of perfection, especially so after the deep fissures inflicted and rigidities produced by the war, and also in view of the self-sufficiency and technical superiority of the American economy. The potential imbalances in international payments, if heavy unemployment was not to be tolerated, were likely to be so large as to render derisory the contemplated volume of additional international liquidity to be provided through the I.M.F. Keynes sensed the gravity of the problem when he first adopted the idea of a Clearing Union during the war, perhaps in 1942 or 1943. In order to avert the risk of a shortage of liquidity, he originally provided for a very large fund which would grow automatically with the expansion in world trade. Opponents argued that the automatic release of such large amounts of international liquidity might cause too rapid an increase in demand in a hungry world starved of commodities, hence unleashing violent (demand) inflation. This argument prevailed in the United States and the American negotiators forced Keynes to concede increasingly stringent limitations and conditions on the availability of additional reserves.[5]

Thus the I.M.F. emerged with its restrictive philosophy. At the end Keynes defended his concessions to the American view by arguing that safeguards had been built into the system to prevent the emergence of large imbalances. These comprised:

(1) The imposition of quotas on imports by countries in balance-of-payments difficulties, in accordance with the rules laid down in the plans for the International Trade Organization (later the General Agreement on Tariffs and Trade);

(2) Mandatory controls over exports of capital by countries making use of their quotas to purchase foreign currencies;[6] and

(3) The scarce-currency clause, which was to permit debtor countries to ration payments for the exports of a country in persistent surplus and thus to restore the basic current balance of payments by direct action.[7]

Much play was made of each of these safeguards at the time. Unfortunately for the supporters of Bretton Woods these ingenious contrivances, which were designed not only to reduce the size of probable imbalances but also to accelerate their adjustment, turned out to be useless, as some of us predicted.[8]

Every single one of these safeguards was eventually to be consigned to oblivion. As for (1), the imposition of quotas was avoided by Britain in 1964 and by the United States in 1971. Instead a much less forceful measure, the import surcharge, was introduced,[9] and subsequently removed before the position had become solidified. As for (2), Mr. Jenkins's Letter of Intent indicated, at a time when Britain was receiving large-scale assistance from the I.M.F. in 1968, that the I.M.F., the Bank of England and, possibly, the Treasury regarded as obsolete the mandatory rule requiring control over capital exports when a country was borrowing from the I.M.F. In an answer to a Parliamentary Question years later, the government spokesman stated that the prohibition on the use of such borrowings to sustain persistent capital exports (Article VI, Section 1(a)) had been relaxed by the Executive Board of the Fund on 28 July 1961.[10] This robs the Fund of one of its most important safeguards and one on which Keynes had laid special emphasis.[11] There is no analogous provision in the Special Drawing Rights scheme.

Finally the scarce-currency clause, which on paper seemed a most potent instrument, has never been invoked. In the decisive early post-war years it could not be used against the United States because, although individual countries were short of dollars, the *Fund itself was not.*[12] In the 1960s, when the Fund was short of Deutsche Marks and the clause could have been invoked, the Americans, still thinking as a creditor country, prevented this from happening. Those British economists—and they were an overwhelming majority, including Sir Roy Harrod, for example—who placed such extravagant hopes in the clause in fact never understood its meaning.[13]

When the first testing time came, in 1947, the Fund was completely by-passed—on American insistence, but also with their generous assistance. Clearly the powers and provisions of the Fund were inadequate, in that the notorious scarce-currency clause could never have worked without American consent. Yet the dollars available to the Fund were quite sufficient to satisfy the severely limited drawing rights of other member countries.

Fortunately the economic crisis had supervened at a time when the Russians were showing signs of becoming aggressive. The Americans, therefore, intervened in order to prevent any severe disruption which might have involved mass unemployment and even a breakdown of the economic order in Western Europe. In the event Marshall Aid represented a vastly greater amount than the original dollar resources of the I.M.F. Even more important, the strict rules of the Fund, based as they were on an unrealistic conception of international economic relations (and which contributed to the crisis), were suspended. The United States even consented to discrimination against its own exports. Thus was a relapse into the pre-war type of business cycle avoided at a critical juncture.

The I.M.F. continued to be by-passed until 1956, again mainly on American insistence. Soon thereafter it was recognized that the means at the disposal of the Fund were insufficient. The quotas were twice increased —in 1958 by 50 per cent, and in 1965 by a further 25 per cent. In addition special adjustments were made to increase the quotas of countries like Germany and Japan into line with their more recent (as against pre-rehabilitation) importance.

These measures were taken as a means of alleviating the rigidity of the original scheme,[14] which, unlike Keynes's proposals, contained no provision for the automatic expansion of its resources. It was hoped that they would provide a durable solution. Yet hardly had they been ratified than the Fund once more took second place in the provision of international liquidity even as stocks of monetary gold began to shrink. Clearly more drastic reforms were needed.

A number of proposals were advanced with a view to modifying the operation of the Fund but, in one way or another, they did not amount to anything more than a stretching of the existing framework; that is, they were directed at providing for a *steady* addition to the increase (judged to be insufficient) in the world's gold and foreign-exchange reserves.[15] How-ever, reserves increased rapidly (see Table 1). Indeed there was a relative abundance, if not surfeit, of reserves. But inasmuch as this expansion was a function of the massive increase in the liquid liabilities primarily of the United States, it undermined confidence in the dollar itself and in the viability of the entire international monetary system as it had developed

TABLE 1. WORLD RESERVES: 1948–71 (III)*
(U.S. $ billion)

	1948	1955	1960	1965	1970	1971 (III)
Gold	32.6	35.4	38.1	41.9	37.2	36.2
of which U.S.A.	24.4	21.8	17.8	14.1	11.1	10.2
Foreign exchange	13.3	19.0	19.0	23.8	44.5	68.9
of which U.S. liabilities	3.4†	8.3	11.1	15.8	23.9	45.7
I.M.F. positions	n.a.	1.0	3.6	5.4	7.7	6.3
S.D.R. allocations	—	—	—	—	3.1	5.9
Total reserves	45.9	56.3	60.7	71.0	92.5	111.3
of which U.S.A.	25.8	22.8	19.4	15.5	14.5	12.1

Source. International Monetary Fund, *International Financial Statistics* (monthly), various issues.

*End-of-period figures, excluding holdings of international agencies.

†Figure refers to 1949.

since the post-war settlement. This loss of confidence was in turn responsible for the drain of official gold reserves into private hoards, a drain which was accelerated by public support by the French government in favour of an increase in the price of gold (especially in terms of the dollar). This was particularly so while the so-called Gold Pool was still in operation.

In general, however, there was little appreciation of this fundamental change much before 1970 or 1971. And even then, as we have seen, America's dominant industrial position gave a peculiar twist to developments in this field. Already before this, and after much haggling—during which the (debtor) Anglo-Saxon countries had pressed for drastic action, while the (mainly creditor) continental countries had urged for more closely circumscribed reforms, reforms which would duly acknowledge their superior states as creditors—a compromise scheme was accepted in principle. This was based on the creation of a new international means of payment, the so-called Special Drawing Rights, the first allocations of which were made on 1 January 1970.

While it is formally no more than a sort of credit scheme, the S.D.R. system can be regarded as the first beginnings of the conscious creation of *owned* as opposed to borrowed international liquidity and, hence, as a new phase in the struggle for a rational, as against mystical, approach to international monetary problems. This follows from the fact that the S.D.R.s are backed by the credit (or rather the currency-issuing power) of all participating countries, in that they undertake to provide domestic currency in exchange for them. Unlike conventional reserves, therefore, their increase is consciously willed and not dependent on a reserve-currency country's 'unfavourable' overall balance of payments. On the contrary, their creation allows other countries to run deficits to help the 'adjustment' process. Unlike ordinary I.M.F. quotas, however, S.D.R.s may be counted as part of a country's reserves; thus an allocation of newly created S.D.R.s will constitute a net addition to world reserves. Moreover, their 'reconstitution', that is repayment (insisted upon by France and certain other continental countries), does not in principle detract from their status as owned reserves. This will therefore obviate the need for creditors to accept a current balance-of-payments deficit in order to overcome the difficulties of persistent debtors in securing a surplus. Without an increase in owned reserves the basis of a steady expansion would be lacking. (Even the extreme monetarist school concede that a steady expansion of 'money' on the international plane, that is, of internationally acceptable reserves, is needed.) At the same time the augmentation of international reserves is determined by common consent and not by the fiat or default of the reserve-currency country. In addition a number of variants of this scheme have been proposed, including the so-called 'link', to help the poorer countries by allocating to them special quotas of S.D.R.s which they may use for purposes of development.[16] The total of S.D.R.s to be credited was initially set at $9,500 billion over three years, which is equivalent to some 7 per cent of the liquid reserves of the West. So far so good.

Where the S.D.R. scheme has shown defects from the very beginning is in its relative rigidity; in the obligation to repay (reconstitution), which reduces some 30 per cent of the original allocation of the status of borrowed reserves; in the slowness of the mechanism of enlarging the amounts available; and in the lack of discretionary powers for the creation of exceptional (large) sums to stifle crises of confidence. After the acceptance of the scheme the world still lacked an international lender of last resort. Indeed, the 1970–1 crisis, which led to the unilateral suspension of convertibility of the dollar by the United States (potentially so disruptive of international trade and payments), has shown that the scheme, as it exists, is quite unfit to cope with crises arising from a general loss of confidence in a major currency, however silly the arguments or rumours that may engender them.

(b) *Abundance of reserves and the marasmus of the dollar*

The Bretton Woods institutions had been conceived at a time when a reversal in the creditor position of the United States seemed unthinkable. Apart from the Swiss franc, the dollar was the only currency with solid backing—as gold is understood in banking circles. It was for this rather archaic reason, and because the dollar was convertible into gold at least as far as foreign governments and central banks were concerned, that the dollar became both the international unit of account and intervention currency of the I.M.F. and of its member countries, not excluding (despite General de Gaulle's hatred of it) the countries of the Common Market. This was certainly not, as some authors have suggested, a lucky coincidence.[17]

Apart from the attendant prestige, the central position of the dollar, as in the case of sterling before it, conferred inestimable advantages on the key-currency country. None the less, the system was dependent for its smooth functioning on a sufficiently large current-account surplus to maintain a credible balance of liquidity.[18] No doubt the gold-exchange standard on which it was based also vouchsafed benefits on the peripheral countries: it enabled them, as we have mentioned,[19] to carry liquid reserves without suffering a total loss of income by so doing (or, indeed, incurring actual costs in storing gold). Nevertheless, the augmentation of liquid liabilities (in effect claims on the key-currency country) must, given the psychology of the international financial and banking fraternity, ultimately undermine the credibility of a key-currency system if it is not accompanied by an increase in assets of similar liquidity.[20]

In due course it became clear that the United States had lost its perennial overall international payments surplus and, indeed, that it was suffering from a steadily increasing deficit. But this deterioration was not brought about by the orthodox equilibrating mechanism of Hume's law at its conventional best,[21] as has been alleged even by Professor Kaldor. It was not 'high living' that wrought the change in the dollar.[22] Rather it was the deliberate exploitation of its role in the international system to defray current government expenditure abroad, to obtain resources and to accumulate high-income-bearing assets against paper obligations of steadily depreciating value. It was the result of military and corporate megalomania, superficially not unlike those problems underlying Britain's own sterling crises.

In Britain too the startling deterioration in its liquidity position was mainly the result of vast private investments abroad, followed by current-account deficits mainly as a consequence of increasing military expenditure. Between 1952 and 1970 Britain's gross exports of private long-term capital amounted to a cumulative total of £6.7 billion, with official government long-term lending adding a further £1.3 billion, and grants of various kinds another £1.9 billion. On the other hand, these outflows were only partially balanced by a cumulative surplus on current account of some £3.2 billion.[23] The United States, on the other hand, not to be outdone, exported some $58.5 billion of private long-term capital and a further $55.4 billion in respect of government lending and grants, against a cumulative current-account surplus of $59.5 billion.[24] In each case, and despite large inflows of *long*-term capital, both countries were forced to borrow *short* in order to lend long—a sure recipe for future trouble.

Yet there was an immense difference. The United States, first of all, started from a position of enormous strength; even in 1965 she was still earning a current-account surplus of $6.2 billion,[25] while Britain since the war has never secured a comfortable current-account surplus simultaneously with a satisfactory level of domestic activity and employment. On the contrary, Britain's post-war progress has been marked by one crisis after another— 1947, 1949, 1951, 1955, 1957, 1961, 1964, 1966–7 and 1971—five under the Tories and four under Labour. In the second place, international economic relations bulk much larger in the British than in the American system. In Britain, visible and invisible exports amount to all but 30 per cent of G.N.P., whereas in the United States the same proportion is a relatively tiny 6.4 per cent. If foreign trade and payments, therefore, are of vital importance to Britain, they are a trifling matter for the United States. Yet the United States accounts for some 15 per cent of the world's exports of manufactures[26] and more than a half of foreign direct investment. Nor is this all.

Overseas assets owned by American corporations now reflect an enormous proportion of the world's productive capacity in the most dynamic and advanced sectors of mining and manufacturing industry—and their growth has been torrential. At the end of 1948, private direct American investment abroad amounted to $9.6 billion, with a further $5.1 billion in foreign portfolio holdings; by the end of 1970 these had increased to $78.1 billion and $26.6 billion, respectively. In the same period, however, while liquid assets had fallen from $19.4 billion to $16.7 billion, liquid liabilities had increased from $21.5 billion to $43.2 billion.[27]

TABLE 2. INTERNATIONAL INVESTMENT POSITION OF THE UNITED STATES:
1948–70
(U.S. $ billion)

	1948	1953	1960	1965	1970
Total foreign assets					
Gross	29.4	39.5	85.6	120.4	166.6
Net	12.9	15.8	44.7	61.6	69.1
Direct investments					
By the United States	9.6	16.2	31.9	49.5	78.1
In the United States	2.8	3.7	6.9	8.8	13.2
Portfolio investments					
By the United States	5.1	5.9	12.7	21.9	26.6
In the United States	3.9	5.5	11.5	17.5	31.6

Source. U.S. Department of Commerce, *Survey of Current Business,* 34 (May 1954) p. 12, Table 2; and *Survey,* 51 (October 1971) p. 21, Table 3.

It was not only on private account that the dollar drain was causing such a drastic deterioration in America's external payments position. Government purchases of goods and services had risen from $13.3 billion in 1939 to $219.4 billion in 1970 (an increase of more than 300 per cent in real terms).[28] Of this, total defence expenditure had risen from $1.2 billion to more than $4.8 billion; and to this must be added a further outflow of $2.0 billion in respect of government loans and grants.[29]

These developments could not, indeed did not, go unnoticed and, in fact, gave rise to a growing political unease. Indeed, resistance to the increasingly widespread expatriate American ownership of the world's most important growth industries, acquired against steadily depreciating dollar balances, should not be underestimated as a factor in hastening the end of confidence and acquiescence in—and, hence, the stability of—the key-currency system. In a critical review of Keynes's posthumously published article[30] on the outlook for America's balance of payments, I wrote:

> There remains the possibility of the United States using her overwhelming investment capacity to mitigate the inequality of the present distribution of

the riches of the world by foreign investment. In the circumstances the maintenance of favourable economic conditions at home and abroad would seem to imply a steady excess of exports over imports of at least $5–10 billion per annum rising with the increase in the United States' national income. In other words the United States would have to lend $5–10 billion while reinvesting repayments and that part of the interest payments which does not give rise to internal consumption. . . . To envisage these orders of magnitude is sufficient to accept them as a *reductio ad absurdum*. . . . Nor would it be permitted by the borrowers themselves, who would pass under an absentee economic domination of the United States which would become politically and socially quite intolerable.[31]

No doubt it could be argued that the increase in American investment abroad, bringing with it a growth in managerial ability and technical know-ledge, was to be welcomed; this was certainly the view of the British government, and especially of the Board of Trade. But in most countries, notably France, Canada and Australia, the reaction was less favourable. Insistent voices were heard that the key-currency system enabled both the United States and Britain to live (invest) beyond their means and to exercise undue economic or political influence.[32]

The pound first, and then the dollar, came under attack. In the spring of 1968 France resumed her deliberate conversion of dollars into gold, thus bringing to a new climax her offensive against the dollar. Within a few months, however, matters were to take a rather different course. The 'events of May' were to herald a massive speculation against the franc (coming to a head in November), while at the same time sterling was feeling the pressure of an anticipated revaluation of the Deutsche Mark. The associated drain on the dollar and, particularly, sterling, although dangerously large, would have been even worse, had it not been for the operations of the central banks[33] which, at the instance of their governments, had been building up throughout the decade a complex framework of currency support agreements.[34] Three months after the Washington agreement of March 1968, however, which, apart from dissolving the Gold Pool had provided additional lines of credit for Britain, sterling came under serious pressure. Disaster was just averted by the announcement in July of standby credits to the amount of $2 billion by the Bank of International Settlements and the Group of Ten at Basle. Later, in November, when the franc was in dire straits the Group of Ten, meeting in Bonn, announced a similar standby credit for France.

Since all these matters were being handled under their aegis, the central banks were succeeding in regaining much of the standing and influence which they had lost during and immediately after World War II. Unfortunately the central banks had during this period also encouraged the development of the Eurocurrency markets, thus not only making it difficult (if not impossible) to identify the origin or limit the extent—and therefore the actual movement—of speculative funds, but also facilitating their rapid multiplication.[35] While these various agreements in effect took upon themselves the task of taming speculative attacks, the policy of re-lending speculative balances ensured their failure. But, in so far as they succeeded, the part played by the I.M.F. was once again reduced to relative insignificance.

These arrangements, however, also permitted the maintenance of exchange rates which were becoming increasingly compromised by divergent cost increases and by consequential speculative anticipations. Had they been followed up by a restoration of balance, preferably by some means acting on both creditor and debtor countries, this would have avoided a too hasty rate of liquidation. As it turned out, the imbalance in the payments position was exacerbated by a dangerous extension (re-cycling) of short-term credit, resulting in the accumulation of a vast quantity of short-term liabilities.

Meanwhile, orthodox opinion, ranging from M. Jacques Rueff in France to Sir Leslie O'Brien, the Governor of the Bank of England, had been aimed at ending this cumulative movement by enforcing a substantial (that is 100 to 200 per cent) increase in the dollar-price of gold, at the same time liquidating the gold-exchange standard based on the dollar. This would have meant effecting an appreciation of all other currencies relative to the dollar and a sufficiently large increase in the dollar-value of American gold reserves so as to be able to pay off dollar liabilities. It is not quite clear how the ensuing paper losses on the dollar reserves of these central banks in terms of gold and other currencies would have been dealt with; presumably the price of gold in terms of other currencies would also have had to be very substantially increased (though not by as much as that in terms of the dollar) in order to equalize them. As we shall see, this was the pattern of the 'solution' reached in 1971, although on a far more modest scale.[36]

As we have seen, the first trial of strength took place in the spring of 1968. At this point the Americans totally resisted—with the effective help of the British Labour Government. They threatened to suspend gold payments and managed to evolve a system which successfully isolated central-bank gold reserves from 'free', outside, gold'hoarded by speculators. In March 1968 they enforced the dissolution of the Gold Pool, the instrument for stabilizing the price of gold in the London market at the official price of $35 per ounce. Sales of gold to private buyers at the official rate was thereafter suspended and the leakage of reserve gold into private hoards staunched.

In thus maintaining the official price of gold at that juncture, and successfully preventing other central banks from selling in the free market despite the initially high premium of 25 per cent,[37] the first step had been taken towards establishing an international monetary system based on a non-metallic reserve medium. But this interim arrangement was not to last. America's overall deficit continued to grow, first with the deterioration in her current balance and, in the absence of effective controls, subsequently as a result of a flight of capital before which earlier sterling crises paled by comparison.

The United States at first tried to prevail upon her competitors (especially Germany and Japan) to revalue their currencies in terms of the dollar and so to avoid the risk of a spate of competitive devaluations. Their response was extremely slow as, all the while, they loudly protested the need for American retrenchment.[38] Meanwhile pressure on American gold reserves, and of Japanese and German competition on American trade, continued to mount.

TABLE 3. BALANCE OF PAYMENTS OF THE UNITED STATES: 1956–71
(U.S. $ million)

	1956	1962	1966	1969	1970	1971*
Merchandise†	4,753	4,561	3,927	660	2,110	−1,744
Military transactions	−2,788	−2,449	−2,935	−3,341	−3,370	−2,735
Investment income:						
Private‡	2,454	3,920	5,331	5,820	6,360	8,248
Government	40	132	44	155	−118	−752
Travel and transport	−361	−1,155	−1,382	−1,780	−1,979	−2,184
Other services	47	140	315	497	587	753
Balance on goods and services	4,145	5,150	5,300	2,011	3,591	1,586
Remittances, pensions and other unilateral transfers†	−2,423	−2,631	−2,890	−2,910	−3,148	−3,364
Current account balance	1,722	2,519	2,410	−899	443	−1,778
Balance on current and long-term capital account	n.a.	−979	−1,614	−2,879	−3,039	−10,162
Balance on liquidity basis	n.a.	−2,864	−2,148	−6,084	−3,821	−23,439
Balance on official reserve transactions basis	n.a.	−2,650	219	−2,702	−9,821	−31,180

Source. *Economic Report of the President* (Washington: United States Government Printing Office, January 1972), Appendix B, Table B–87.

*Average of the first three quarters on a seasonally adjusted annual rates basis.

†Excludes military grants.

‡Includes fees and royalties from U.S. direct investments abroad or from foreign direct investment in the United States.

Moreover, an increasingly (if belatedly) obvious menace was the prospective entry into the Common Market of four countries (especially Britain), a development that would extend to what had been the world's largest and most stable international market for foodstuffs and certain raw materials the most far-reaching protection.[39]

In the autumn of the following year the new German Coalition Government, taking heart from the result of the election in September 1969—which they had won, despite the decision to float a few days earlier—officially revalued the Deutsche Mark by some $9\frac{1}{4}$ per cent. In May 1971 the Mark was again allowed to float, and by August had appreciated a further 8 per cent against the dollar. The Japanese on the other hand resolved not to budge, absorbing dollars the while at an incredible rate. While Japan's current-account surplus soared from $2 billion in 1970 to $5.9 billion in 1971 its official reserves increased in the same year by more than $10 billion, to $14.6 billion (that is, by almost 300 per cent). Clearly the Americans could not tolerate the further consequential pressure on their employment or the accumulation of 'debts' which could not possibly be met in terms of acceptable assets. That these losses were to a large extent due to longer-term investment and short-term capital flight—which could (and should) have been dealt with by direct measures—was an awkward, if most important, feature of the crisis, but which a Conservative Administration, however, was at pains not to stress.

Finally the unbelievable happened. A *Republican* President suspended the convertibility of the dollar, while at the same time taking a number of protectionist steps calculated to limit American imports and to stimulate exports. With these measures the whole picture was transformed and the onus of intervening to prevent the dollar from depreciating shifted from the debtor country on to the creditors; if they allowed the dollar to fall the American balance of trade and services would in principle improve.[40]

But a sudden change in American exports and an improvement in the international competitiveness of the American economy might spell ruin for its industrial rivals in the most advanced and science-based sectors overseas. An export surplus for the United States, while small, possibly, in terms of its own national product, might have serious implications for others. There can be no doubt on the particular point that the generation of an export surplus big enough to allow the United States to cover its present military activities and civilian investment in the advanced countries abroad would far exceed anything that could in practice (if not in principle) be compatible with full employment in those areas, and thus acceptable to her trading partners.

It is from this vantage point that the tactics of the United States in 1971 have to be judged. The Americans had been under pressure since 1968 to devalue the dollar in terms of gold. This they countered by asking their principal competitors rather to revalue their currencies in terms of the dollar, and finally, through President Nixon's policy revolution of 15 August, by forcing them to agree to a general resettlement of monetary affairs.

Hardly had the equanimity of the central-banking community been shattered than they tried desperately—and with the aid of the American conservative-'liberal' economists[41]—to get the United States to restore the convertibility of the dollar, to suspend the 'protectionist' measures, and yet also to restore balance to their international payments.[42] Once again, however, it was demonstrated that under a régime of non-convertibility the bargaining position of debtor countries becomes superior to that of creditors. The Americans rightly insisted that the problems of foreign trade—and especially those which arose in connection with the enlargement of the E.E.C.—had to be treated as a package with that of exchange rates. In this way, and only in this way, could the general rearrangement of currencies be obtained. At the same time, a régime of non-convertibility was repugnant to orthodox conservatives, and it was this which presumably induced President Nixon partially at least to capitulate to the Six (reinforced by Britain) even before the vital talks on commercial relations had taken place.

A compromise agreement was ultimately reached at a meeting of the Group of Ten at the Smithsonian Institute of all places on 17–18 December 1971, in which the Americans, while conceding little, obtained concessions themselves which their competitors had not previously contemplated. The issues agreed comprised:

(1) The establishment of a new pattern of fixed (so-called 'central') rates of exchange—mainly to the advantage of the United States—under which the Japanese yen and the Deutsche Mark were to move up *vis-à-vis* the dollar by 16.9 and 13.6[43] per cent, respectively, while the French and British parities were to remain the same in terms of gold, thus implying a revaluation against the dollar of 8.6 per cent (see (4));

(2) The widening of the permissible band of fluctuation from 1 to $2\frac{1}{4}$ per cent on either side of the new 'central' rates;

(3) The removal of the 10 per cent surcharge on American imports imposed on 15 August 1971, as well as of the export subsidies granted by way of tax-credits for investments; and

(4) An increase in the official price of gold from \$35 to \$38 per ounce subject to Congressional ratification (this being mainly a concession to the French).

The last point was, of course, a purely formal gesture, since it did not entail, nor was it followed by, the restoration of the convertibility of the dollar, either into gold or other reserve assets (whether S.D.R.s or foreign exchange, e.g. Deutsche Marks). It remained, in other words, with the rest of the world to preserve, as before, the new exchange rate of the dollar by their willingness to purchase any amounts of dollars that happened to come on to the market.

While the rest of the Group of Ten (with the exception of Canada), representing the overwhelming proportion of world trade in manufactures and of world payments, had agreed on a new system of fixed exchange rates, there had as yet been no decision on the linchpin of the agreement, the character and management of the reserve unit. What had been achieved, therefore, was nothing like 'the most significant monetary agreement in the history of the world', as President Nixon called it.

The changes in currency values agreed in Washington are discrete, once-for-all, at least in the short term, while the problems which create the need for recurrent adjustments in exchange rates are continuous, persistent and cumulative. Moreover, the marked behavioural differences between leading countries, differences which are institutionally and historically determined, and their influence on the pattern of cost movements, create periodically recurrent imbalances which become exaggerated by capital flows. Unless these institutional differences can be constrained within tolerable limits the continued recurrence of these problems must create insupportable difficulties.

This episode, if it serves no other purpose, must surely drive home the point once and for all that international economic relations are by nature oligopolistic and that the game of bluff and counter-bluff in which dominant countries indulge with their weaker counterparts necessarily gives rise to historically unique situations. The events of the last few years, culminating in the agreement of December 1971, have nothing to do with the sterile apersonality of perfectly competitive theoretical models, whether Keynesian or monetarist. Indeed, the aftermath of the Smithsonian agreement is clear testimony to the destructive consequences that may follow from the thoughtless application of neo-classical remedies without sufficient prior diagnosis of prevailing conditions. Especially relevant here is the traditional view that a widening of the permissible range of exchange-rate fluctuations would abate the damaging ebb and flow of short-term (hot) funds.[44] Clearly the realignments mentioned, together with the widening of the band to $4\frac{1}{2}$ per cent, have not solved the problem of achieving stability in the international monetary sphere. Thus, while President Nixon's measures aimed at freezing prices and wages and the institution of a long-term policy on prices and incomes have been successful in reducing the domestic rate of inflation in the United States,[45] international speculative movements continued, indeed intensified.

First it was the turn of the dollar to come under renewed pressure. During the first two months of the new year (1972) the exchange reserves of the rest of the Group of Ten increased by $2.3 billion which, with the exception of December 1971 itself, was at least as massive an inflow as in any of the three or four months preceding the agreement. The weakness of the dollar, which went through its worst patch in early March, was reflected in the temporary strength of the pound, which at one stage rose to $2.65, only 1 cent below its new official ceiling.

TABLE 4. GOLD AND EXCHANGE RESERVES OF THE GROUP OF TEN*
(U.S. $ billion)

End of period	Gold and exchange	Change + or −	(of which exchange)	(Change + or −)
1970 4th Quarter	38.3		21.2	
1971 1st „	42.3	+4.0	26.0	+4.8
2nd „	45.7	+3.4	29.4	+3.4
3rd „	55.2	+9.5	38.8	+9.4
4th „	61.5	+6.3	43.7	+4.9
1972 1st „	64.4	+2.9	46.7	+3.0
1971 August	54.0		37.6	
September	55.2	+1.2	38.8	+1.2
October	56.1	+0.9	39.7	+0.9
November	57.6	+1.5	41.2	+1.5
December	61.5	+3.9	43.7	+2.5
1972 January	61.6	+0.1	44.4	+0.7
February	63.2	+1.6	46.0	+1.6
March	64.4	+1.2	46.7	+0.7
April	65.6	+1.2	47.6	+0.9
May	65.0	−0.6	47.2	−0.4

Source. International Monetary Fund, *International Financial Statistics* (monthly), various issues.
*Excluding the United States.

But it was the pound itself that was next in the line of fire. Barely six months after the Smithsonian realignment, and only six weeks since Britain had joined the 'snake in the tunnel',[46] the new central rate of the pound had become untenable. After a week or so of violent speculation, beginning in mid-June, some $2,600 million worth of E.E.C. support had failed to restrict the value of the pound within the snake's 2¼ per cent band, and on 23 June it was effectively floated. Indeed, at $2.525, the pound had even left the tunnel.[47] Thereafter the pound continued to float sharply downwards towards its previous parity, reaching its low point at $2.4125 in early July, whence it recovered (presumably as a result of the float being 'slightly 'dirty') to fluctuate around $2.44 and $2.45, representing an effective devaluation against the dollar of about 6½ per cent. It was during this period also that the lira came under attack, though not so much from international speculators as from the illegal export of Italian banknotes by residents. Accordingly, Italy's Common Market partners agreed to a special authorization under which for a period of three months dollars rather than other reserve components might be used to defend a run on the lira.

Meanwhile the relief for the pound had only been temporary. By mid-October the pressure had been renewed and was subsequently to carry it to its lowest recorded level of $2.32 (at which time also a new attack was brewing against the dollar, especially *vis-à-vis* the yen). For this persistent weakness of the pound the most likely cause was the compounded influence of two related factors: first, the anticipation of speculators that there would be a further sharp devaluation preparatory to the fixing of a new parity on entry into the Common Market, even before the problem of internal stability had been settled; and secondly, the fact that growing inflationary pressure had once more undermined Britain's international competitiveness.

Obviously, there is as yet no solution in sight. Indeed, the 'agenda' adopted at the Smithsonian meeting was clearly one-sided.[48] The Americans —unlike most contemporary British experts, but like their British nineteenth-century forerunners—were quick to adapt themselves as soon as their position as a (short-term) debtor had become clear to them at last. Mr. George Shultz, the new (conciliatory) Secretary of the Treasury,[49] having refused to budge on convertibility, defended the American position almost as uncompromisingly as his (aggressive) predecessor, Mr. George Connally:

> Building upon the Smithsonian Agreement, we can now seek a firm consensus for new monetary arrangements that will serve us all in the decades ahead. Indeed, I believe certain principles underlying monetary reform already command widespread support. . . . First is our mutual interest in encouraging freer trade in goods and services and the flow of capital to the places where it can contribute most to economic growth. . . . Surpluses in payments are too often regarded as a symbol of success and of good management rather than as a measure of the goods and services provided from a nation's output without current return. . . . Freer trade must be reconciled with the need for each country to avoid abrupt change involving serious disruption of production and employment. . . . A second fundamental is the need to develop a common code of conduct to protect and strengthen the fabric of a free and open international economic order. . . . Such basic rules as 'no competitive devaluation' and 'most-favoured nation treatment' . . . need to be reaffirmed. . . . We must recognize the need for clear disciplines and standards of behaviour to guide the international adjustment process. . . . Effective and symmetrical incentives for adjustment are essential to a lasting system. . . . The belief is widespread—and we share it—that the exchange rate system must be more flexible. . . . As we seek to reform monetary rules, we must at the same time seek to build in incentives for trade liberalization. . . . Any stable and well-functioning international monetary system must rest upon sound policies to promote domestic growth and price stability in the major countries.[50]

These precepts are excellent as far as they go, although not always acknowledged during America's unrecondite creditor phase. Yet they still fail to recognize certain simple but important facts. In the first place, the present open system of world trade depends on the ability to check inflationary pressures of more than average intensity by means of policies which do not necessitate large-scale unemployment and the consequent repercussions that this would imply for the developing countries. As we shall see, the assumption of symmetry and the view that capital movements are 'balancing', or that they can be checked by allowing a wider band of fluctuation between the intervention points of currency parities, are wholly unwarranted. For these reasons far more drastic powers are required than have been contemplated by the reformed and debtor-minded United States.

It would be interesting, perhaps, to conclude this section with some words concerning France (and, under her leadership, the rest of the E.E.C.), whose position in all this has been, to say the least, intriguing. Throughout these dealings—indeed well before the advent of the present crisis—the French had been pursuing a double policy of trying to 'depose' the dollar from its position as intervention currency and to impose on the United States a painful (that is, deflation-induced) readjustment of her balance of payments. But in a speech given at Bordeaux in the summer of 1972 by the Governor of the Bank of France, M. Olivier Wormser, it is shown clearly that the French did not appreciate that these twin ambitions are incompatible, since the scale of the reversal required to remove America's deficit could only result in a strengthening of the dollar's position in world markets; so far from being deposed, the dollar's status as intervention currency would be enhanced by its renewed scarcity.

Moreover, the French, in their reluctance to revalue and in their atavistic insistence on a substantial increase in the dollar-price of gold, seem to have been unaware that, by so increasing the extent of the American adjustment that would have to be accomplished by deflationary means, they would be putting their own prosperity at risk. But when the French have pursued such inconsistent policies before. In 1930–1 they opposed aid to Germany; in 1932–3 they favoured deflation; and did they not during 1933–6, as the leading member of the Gold Bloc (that monument to monetary primitivism), suffer a worse and longer stagnation than any other industrial country in the world?[51] At any rate, this latest folly was scotched when the Americans suspended convertibility.[52]

The other tactic in the scheme to dethrone the dollar, of course, has been to establish a monetary union in the E.E.C. Yet here again, disregard for the real implications of a union of unequal partners has gone hand in hand with an extreme irritation with the Anglo-Saxon countries and their slovenly approach to economic management.[53]

In February 1969 the first Barré plan was presented to the Council of Ministers[54] and in December of that year the Summit Conference at The Hague proclaimed the objective of establishing a monetary and economic union.[55] Yet for some time thereafter the so-called 'Hague spirit' was little in evidence. The Germans demanded a much closer (and centralized) degree of integration than the French were willing to accept,[56] the latter being determined to circumscribe the role of the Commission. Then the crises of 1970 and 1971, and the parity changes which they precipitated, were a further obstacle on the path of unification. Nevertheless, after repeated agreements had fallen victim to the repercussions of the ailing dollar, further agreement was reached in March 1972 on the implementation of the first stage of integration.[57] As already mentioned, this called for a narrowing of the intervention points of the currencies of the Community (and later Britain) to a limit of $2\frac{1}{4}$ per cent (i.e. to 1.215 per cent on either side of parities), and provided for short-term monetary assistance amounting to $1000 million, a derisory sum if past experience is any guide. (Indeed, Britain's losses exceeded this amount in one afternoon.)

The present agreement, as far as Europe is concerned, carries with it the threat of a repetition of the pattern of imbalances which led to the first breakdown of the Bretton Woods system in 1947. A narrowing of the permissible margin of fluctuation between the currencies of the Community will not displace the dollar; it will merely throw the burden of intervention *vis-à-vis* the dollar on to the strongest currency in the Community—the Deutsche Mark. Any procedure for intra-European clearing implied by such a narrowing of bands will leave a net balance with the United States to be dealt with and since Germany has a positive balance with almost all her Common Market partners it will be on her balance of payments—in effect the net European balance—that the additional burden will fall. With controls over intra-Community capital movements and trade forbidden and parities fixed, this almost certainly implies that Germany, unless she can gain some power of veto over the general economic policies of the rest, will have to extend vastly greater credits than initially envisaged. This power of veto would have to cover not merely the methods and strategy of demand management, but also the establishment of a uniform system of controls over capital movements. The maintenance of a 'second' foreign-exchange market for 'financial' transactions with the outside world, such as was instituted by France, and which was maintained by Belgium for a while, would only be feasible under these conditions if payments from those countries indulging in multiple exchange practices (even to member countries) were supervised. Without such safeguards, however, the chances are that the tragi-comic episode of 1947 (and 1972) will be repeated, but with a different cast and, it is to be feared, without the generous gesture of Marshall Aid being forthcoming.

The British reaction to these moves was clearly guided by the wish of the Prime Minister not to antagonize President Pompidou. Thus at the Summit Meeting of the Community in October 1972 Mr. Heath accepted the French plan to reaffirm and accelerate monetary unification,[58] but without gaining any assurances in respect of the contribution to be made by the Community to the solution of Britain's regional problems: this in the teeth of evidence that Britain's inflationary drift was continuing worse than elsewhere and that the slight *de facto* competitive advantage secured *vis-à-vis* the Common Market countries under the Smithsonian realignment had again been wiped out.[59]

2. INTERNATIONAL READJUSTMENT IN A FRAMEWORK OF OLIGOPOLY: INFLATION, BEGGAR-MY-NEIGHBOUR AND FLEXIBILITY

(a) *The problem of cost-push inflation*

A number of views are held as to the cause, nature and, by implication, permanence of the remarkable transformation of the world economy since World War II, and particularly the international position of the United States. Much the most important aspect of post-war economic history has been the relentless rise in the price of manufactures. Apart from a few exceptions—mainly goods whose production is intensive in the use of raw materials—none has experienced a fall in price, even in periods of relatively high rates of unemployment or unused capacity. I shall argue that most of the payments imbalances and crises that have beset the developed world have been the result of diverging rates of cost inflation; and that the traditional see-saw flows due to excessive demand were the exception. In my view this fact necessitates a drastic rethinking of the requirements of reform.

Among the most important causes of this post-war trend has been the radical change in political attitudes, especially in the Anglo-Saxon countries. Governments have been forced to acknowledge responsibility for maintaining (fullish) employment. Economists have tended to attribute this mainly to Keynes's 'new economics';[60] in my opinion the process was not, perhaps, quite so simple. As we have seen, a vital element consists in a deep-seated malaise, the seeds of which were planted by the menace of military and corporate megalomania, and the almost ubiquitous change both in the structure of industry and in the organization of labour; a further element was the experience of wartime full employment.[61] This is not to discount entirely the impact of the victorious Keynesian revolution on political attitudes; yet, when set in the perspective of the rise of massive counter-forces in the economic, political and social spheres, the apotheosis of Keynes assumes increasingly the attributes of myth rather than substance.

Keynes's open-ended framework of analysis[62] did not in the least accord with the scientific aspirations of his followers in the conversion from orthodoxy. What it implied was the necessity for an historical and sociological approach to economics and economic policy-making. This no economist, priding himself on his capacity to form objective and quantifiable judgements, could stomach. The so-called Keynesian 'synthesis', which for a time swept the academic board, was soon accomplished by Keynes's liberal disciples. With but marginal modifications the neo-classical theory of social harmony and income distribution was reconnected to the newly erected macro-economic edifice, in which the automatism of the market economy, with its assurance of full employment and optimal resource allocation, was simply replaced by the twin *deus ex machina* of the Treasury and the Central Bank.

At the precise time when markets were being increasingly dominated by national and international oligopoly power, theoretical orthodoxy ensured that the very problem to which this would give rise would be ignored or dismissed.[63] The self-consistency and determinacy of the system was completed by the idea that politicians could choose at their discretion the level of unemployment at which the economy should be operated, and that this level would be an expression of the will of the community, dependent mainly, if not entirely, on the amount of inflation which would be accepted.

What was gained from the point of view of professional and political respectability was lost by the increasingly manifest inability of the 'new' doctrine to account for actual developments. It gained acceptance because its formulation was ultimately deeply conservative in character. Its adherents believed that our economic problems could be solved by painless gadgets so long as the number of policy instruments in the fiscal and monetary field corresponded to the number of policy objectives, i.e. Tinbergen's so-called law.[64] The current neo-Keynesian case, then, is conducted not in terms of the real world with its massive concentrations of economic power, but in terms of the same old imaginary system with its susceptibility to finely calibrated optimal adjustment.

It is characteristic of this apolitical approach to what is fundamentally a purely political problem that even so radical a Keynesian as Professor Kaldor should resist accepting the ineluctable fact of experience that harmony cannot be achieved in a globally managed economic system. For example, in his Presidential Address to the Economic Section of the British Association in 1970, he said:

> The failure of post-war Governments to pursue a policy consistent in terms of its declared objectives could ... be primarily attributed to an insufficient orchestration of instruments. ... If demand management (through fiscal policy) is used to secure the target level of employment, another instrument— which can only be thought of in terms of an incomes policy—is needed to secure the target rate of wage increases; and yet a further instrument—a flexible exchange rate—to secure the target balance of payments.[65]

But he went on:

> As the problem of an incomes policy raises sociological and political issues that are outside my competence, and it is a problem that is common to all industrial countries, and not specific to Britain, I do not propose to consider it today in any detail. Instead I shall devote the rest of this address to the other major problem of economic management—the question of exchange-rate policy.[66]

In brief, Professor Kaldor completely ignores the fact that the policy which he advocates, the successful management of a floating rate of exchange, is at least as much determined by 'sociological and political issues that are outside [his] competence' as is incomes policy, on account of the anticipations of speculators and of the reactions of unions and employers to the consequences of (downward) changes in parity. Incidentally—*pace* Professor Tinbergen's 'well-known principle of the modern theory of economic policy'[67]—a successful incomes policy would not serve merely as a policy instrument to secure relative stability, but at the same time would be politically and psychologically the only feasible method for a 'weak' country to secure external balance; moreover, we should thereby have gone some way in reconciling full employment with stability. As I shall show later, floating is feasible only if the majority do not expect the rate to float consistently downward.[68] This, I fear, however, is a 'sociological and political' issue, because intimately bound up with the same problem and motivations as the issue of incomes policy. Indeed, the persistent underestimation of the importance of evolving an acceptable incomes policy finds its explanation in this failure of understanding. It seems that orthodox Keynesians still neglect the intimate connection between downward changes in exchange rates and wage and price movements.[69]

Nevertheless, in face of the increasingly tight bilateral monopoly relationship in wage determination and the oligopolistic management of prices,[70] even intelligent authors continue their hopeless quest for the determinate economic system, because they will not recognize the vital importance of social and institutional factors which make it impossible to maintain restrictive measures over long periods; an additional factor has been the growing political pressure that has led to a steady increase in government expenditures, especially in periods of increased unemployment. These considerations in turn lead inevitably to the need for a political solution, such as an explicit consensus on incomes.

The liberal–conservative Keynesian belief that all would be well if only demand were stabilized at a level that secured full employment (but no more) has been seen to be virtually meaningless as a policy prescription. Indirect, global, attempts at stabilization, advocated by the anti-interventionist school of thought, have proved ineffectual. Wage demands and price increases have continued to chase each other round an anticipatory spiral; nowhere has price stability been achieved, despite increased unemployment in almost every country, including those with external surpluses. None the less, it is almost certain that a recurrence of old-style crises has only been avoided because of the rather cautious approach to monetary policy adopted by those people who still remember the aftermath of the monetary experiments of Governors Montagu Norman and Benjamin Strong between 1928 and 1933. If, as I argue, prosperity has been achieved since World War II not by the invention and use of new economic weaponry, but by the pressure of wage increases maintaining internal demand, then a new approach to the problem is needed.

The inescapable lesson of the inter-war years is that all indirect policy measures, whether monetary or fiscal, can only operate through their psychological impact. But this necessitates 'overkill', that is, measures are required to be more savage (or vice versa) than is indicated by the 'objective' situation—if such an abstraction from the psychology inextricably bound up with booms and slumps has any meaning—in order to offset the effect, whether optimistic or pessimistic, of the prevailing climate of opinion.[71] No one has ever solved the problem of rising prices by indirect monetary methods, except by inducing a crisis. Historical evidence shows clearly that when such measures 'worked'—and work they did—they worked by destroying optimism in time of boom. The result was pessimism, unemployment, and finally falling prices and wages. Consequently, in order to restore confidence, nothing less than a hefty stimulus was needed, in those days mainly in the form of easing the monetary situation. But later on in the cycle, after business and financial opinion had again become more sanguine, counter-measures were again invariably needed. Changes in mental outlook did not work through a subtle, slow and painless change in costs and incomes; they worked themselves out explosively, destructively and at immense cost in terms of lost output.

Growing affluence, by making people less price-sensitive, and increased taxation, moreover, have steadily reduced the 'non-violent' effectiveness of monetary policy, that is, its impact on costs. This is especially so in respect of interest rates, whose adverse effects on costs (and, hence, profits) can be mitigated by their deductibility against corporate tax assessments. 'Deflationary' fiscal measures, from which so much—i.e. 'fine-tuning'—was expected, can, on the other hand, be offset by the mobilization of assets and reserves, by reducing savings and by increasing wage demands. The existence of vast stocks of durables, the replacement of which could be postponed over long periods, might make a future downswing—if confidence were destroyed—far more destructive than those experienced before the war.[72]

Disappointment with the Keynesian remedies, however, has led to a revival of the crudest form of the so-called Quantity Theory. This alleges that the quantity of money bears a stable relationship with a whole range of operational economic variables such as expenditure, output, income and prices. These relationships, moreover, are claimed to be reversible, with the implication that changes in the volume of money are of supreme relevance for policy-making purposes. After 1955, and more or less closely associated with Dr. Per Jacobsson's period as Managing Director of the I.M.F., bankers and Treasury officials were inclined to rely on at least a modified, but still highly simplistic, version of that theory. The quantity of money became a principal, if not *the* principal, target of policy, and its relation with the earlier Keynesian liberal orthodoxy was maintained (or restored) by attributing to the volume of domestic credit expansion a decisive importance in the determination of the growth of the supply of money. This reflected, however, a hopeless confusion of mind as between changes in asset-holding as a result of changes in the demand for liquidity and actual effective demand.[73]

Here too, however, disillusionment was to be no less acute. Professor Friedman, that high priest of the monetarist cult, has disclaimed (at any rate after some experience with his 'counter-revolutionary' policies) any such close relationship between the volume of money and spending:

> The fact that inflation results from changes in the quantity of money relative to output does not mean that there is a precise, rigid, mechanical relationship between the quantity of money and prices, which is why the weasel-word 'substantial' was sprinkled in my initial statement of the proposition.[74]

But if a policy based on the regulation of the quantity of money is to work smoothly, a close relationship is required, otherwise even a sharp boom might be 'carried' by an accommodating increase in the velocity of monetary circulation which, if it threatened to get out of hand, would have to be followed by further restrictive measures to check it. Only if expenditures were markedly interest-elastic, however, would this type of policy succeed. All post-war experience, however, is in direct conflict with the hypothesis that expenditure changes are closely related to such variations.

If one feature characterizes academic economics, and consequently its failure as a reliable guide in practical affairs, it lies in its persistent striving after determinacy where none exists. The post-war period has seen the most remarkable changes in industrial and market relationships, and no more so than in the immense concentration of power in the hand of a few corporations, and the deliberate manipulation of markets and consumer tastes that that engenders.[75] It should be noted in reference to our earlier remarks, however, that this merely reinforces the view that post-war prosperity has not been a simple legacy of consciously pursued Keynesian policies.

Nor is excess demand a prerequisite of the existence of price inflation as long as all entrepreneurs are confident that other firms will be confronted with similar wage demands, whether simultaneously or at various stages during a given 'wage-round'. Thus, even if individual entrepreneurs alone cannot afford to agree to wage increases—because they cannot recoup their position individually—collectively such wage increases stimulate the demand for each other's products which in turn justifies the required all-round increase in prices—and, hence, restrospectively, in wages. What entrepreneurs cannot afford are strikes, which would interrupt production and menace their survival. Union demands can thus be met irrespective of increases in productivity. It should be stressed, however, that there is no solid evidence that the unions will be successful (except individually and in the very short run) in increasing the share of wages in the national income. [76] The malaise of post-war inflation, which both Keynesians and monetarists alike have failed to explain or account for, has ultimately forced a theoretical reconsideration of the problem, not least because of its explicit threat to the entire accumulation of orthodox wisdom. [77] It is this which unquestionably underlies the most recent appearance of a slightly modified version of pre-Keynesian Austrian trade-cycle theory, whose lunatic logic and unrealistic assumptions caused such confusion and havoc after 1929. At that time, not only baffled neo-classicists in British and American universities, but also high Treasury officials and central bankers all over the world, had been convinced by this 'deep' analysis that public works and other forms of expansionary state intervention would distort the structure of relative prices and that any increase in the 'roundaboutness' of production (as a result of the inflation and consequent 'forced saving') would be a temporary phenomenon, unless sustained by further and repeated stimuli—which, of course, would perpetuate the inflation. [78] Yet, despite a swift and effective (and what ought to have been a conclusive) refutation of these fallacies, [79] we are now treated to a *réchauffé* [80] without so much as a sidelong acknowledgement of earlier objections. The bogey is still the distortion of relative prices, although it is now trade-union monopoly power which frustrates the pristine directive balancing mechanism of the market.

In the new scheme management is absolved of all blame. Since monopoly (or rather oligopoly) in *commodity* markets can no longer be credibly denied its effects are dismissed as a 'one-shot affair' which merely raises the general level of prices above what would have prevailed in a hypothetical state of perfect competition. The true significance of monopoly is disregarded—that once market power has been established, all increases in costs (including wages and interests rates) can be passed on to the consumer. But the new–old school have to reject this. Indeed their theoretical structure would collapse were they to accept that perfect competition (if it ever existed) is a thing of the past. In their view every departure from competition is abnormal, even immoral. Thus these conservative-'liberals' have been reduced to advocating what would amount to a revival of Pitt's Combination Laws. The withdrawal of social benefits from strikers' families and the need for intensified police action against strikers and their pickets would inevitably follow, for, without repressive measures, there can be no prospect of any diminution in the 'monopoly power' of the trade unions.

It need hardly be said that no democratic government could possibly contemplate such a course. Yet there is no doubt either that unrestricted sectional wage bargaining at high levels of employment will continue to lead irresistibly to price increases and, hence, to repeated crises.

The mulish reluctance of the profession to admit the fact that structural changes have rendered the economic system indeterminate and unstable is therefore quite comprehensible.[81] Some, however, do not give up even yet. After due breast-beating, Professor Walters of the London School of Economics, one of those Friedmanites whose monetary explanations have exploded in their faces, admits:

> The desperation with which professional economists (and others) have sought remedies and the variety of policies suggested are some indication of the quandary in which economists find themselves. Not since the early 1930s has there been such uncertainty and disappointment with the standard policy prescriptions. . . . Yet clearly one should not give up the ghost! Surely one can find a pattern and a theory of this adjustment process! The most distinguished monetarist, Milton Friedman, has indeed recently suggested a tentative theory of the adjustment process explicitly incorporating the division of changes in money income between changes in the price level and changes in real output. But he does not specify the determinants of the division between changes in output and prices; nor does he specify the time path.[82]

This may reflect Professor Friedman's audacity, but as 'a theoretical framework for monetary analysis' this is not very convincing.[83] Indeed, it is interesting to note that Professor Friedman himself now seems to have joined the ranks of the penitents and taken to sack-cloth and ashes.[84]

Only lately has there been an unwilling retreat from the light-hearted nonchalance with which downward-floating or exchange-devaluation had come to be relied on as the supreme remedy for stagnation and unemployment in the face of continued inflation.[85] Although Mr. Worswick had been amongst the first (along with others at the old Institute of Statistics in Oxford) to recognize the nature of the new political cycle in economic policy-making,[86] none the less the National Institute has only very recently come to accept the diagnosis of cost-push which even as far back as the first post-war Labour Government had failed to gain acceptance:

> For a long time the conventional wisdom has had it that, given existing institutions and methods of income and price determination, there was a trade-off between unemployment and inflation. The experience of the recent past suggests that the more relevant choice may be between inflation and changing those institutions and methods.[87]

The present British Conservative Government's 'adjustment' policy, in its first phase, can be summed up as a one-sided attempt to keep down wages in the public sector while hoping to be able to manage the economy at large by the use of 'general pressures',[88] that is through classical monetary policy. At the same time, while increases in rents, rates and the prices of other essential goods were adversely affecting the lower-middle income groups, and especially those on sluggishly growing or fixed incomes, the Government granted vast tax concessions which mainly benefited the rich and very rich and introduced means-tested relief for the very poor. This had the effect of exacerbating the so-called 'poverty trap', that is the high marginal loss of relief payments which attends increases in (very low) incomes.[89]

The consequent deterioration in the relations between the Government and the unions in the public sector has a very good economic explanation. Only the public sector can resist strikes for long without risking bankruptcy and, in so far as the Government was successful in its policy of confrontation against the miners, postmen, railwaymen and dustmen, the result was to upset the balance in the structure of wages between the public and private sectors. But so long as such divisive policies were followed—and if our analysis of the nature of cost-push inflation is correct—it is impossible to keep inflation down to a reasonably low rate without resorting to severely repressive social, indeed police, measures in order to weaken the bargaining power of the unions. Ultimately, therefore, the Government was unsuccessful, since it recoiled from carrying its policies to their logical conclusion; and with the policy of resistance to union pressure and general deflation unable to stem the tide, inflation continued to worsen and stagnation became increasingly entrenched.[90]

As unemployment rose to unprecedented post-war levels during 1971 and early 1972,[91] the Government reversed its restrictive monetary policy and permitted a huge increase in the volume of money[92] which, rather than stimulating output, simply created an asset boom, especially in land. In addition, the Chancellor, in his Budget speech in March 1972, declared that he would not sacrifice expansion and employment to the defence of an unrealistic exchange rate.[93] In the circumstances, therefore, the sterling crisis in June was virtually inevitable, and with the decision to float the pound, coming as it did after the Government's defeat at the hands of the miners, railwaymen and dockers, the rate of successfully increased wage demands once more resumed its upward trend.[94]

At this point, Mr. Heath, closely emulating President Nixon's apparently successful tactics, performed a complete volte-face by proposing (albeit voluntary) restraints on prices and wages, although in order to secure popular support in this there was to be an upper absolute limit (rather than a proportionate one) on the amount by which wages and salaries could rise in a given period, irrespective of the level of current earnings. But there was a fatal snag, in that the policies (especially fiscal) which the Government had implemented and were in the process of introducing themselves sharply militated against the possibility of achieving a consensus. Clearly the package proposed by the Government in the autumn of 1972 would have meant a freezing of the existing position. Those who had benefited from the Government's measures to date (and the benefits were substantial) would keep their gains; and the less well off who had suffered would find their burdens unrelieved. Profits, land- and house-prices, and dividends were not on the list of items that were to be subject to control; nor was there any promise that the most objectionable features of the Budget were to be revised. Yet there is no doubt that some solution will have to be found if a rate of inflation of Latin American ferocity is to be avoided.[95]

It is from this point of view that one must judge the Government's failure to secure voluntary agreement and its decision in November 1972 to introduce statutory controls, this time on dividends as well as on prices and wages and salaries. It is by no means certain that even the freezing of an iniquitous situation will not lead to the successful resistance of the unions and perhaps also to a victory for the Conservatives in a General Election on the issue of 'who runs the country?'. In a way the union leaders may well have to pay the price for their lack of co-operation with a Labour Government that was prepared to explore the conditions on which a new social compact on inflation could be founded. For in all Western countries the problem of domestic stability and international equilibrium turns on whether the unions can be brought freely to accept a sufficiently sharply defined incomes policy. This will ultimately depend on whether a general policy package can be formulated such as will tilt the social balance in favour of the lower income groups while retaining a sufficient margin for investment and, moreover, which will confront the individual union membership with overwhelming public opinion in its favour.[96] As yet there is no reason for confidence in this vital matter, despite President Nixon's moderate success in reducing inflation and wage demands.

(b) *Keynesian unemployment: undervaluation as a weapon*

For a long time before the war the industrialized world lived in an atmosphere of acute Keynesian unemployment. This experience has been deeply ingrained in the consciousness of all who suffered, but especially of the Anglo-Saxon countries. Their world has since been dominated, consequently, by governments fearful of defeat, lest the spectre of unemployment reappear. In such circumstances beggar-my-neighbour policies,[97] especially currency devaluations, were prized, although actual devaluation as such seems to have been rather detrimental to the political survival of finance ministers.[98]

Until very recently, therefore, the advantages of keeping the currency undervalued seem to have been regarded as overwhelming, at any rate among 'enlightened' economists. A general consensus that 'overvaluation' should be avoided at *all* costs became established. Not only was it argued to have the merits, as a policy, of being simple and painless in application, but the terrible struggles of British governments of all hues[99] were held up as an awful warning of the consequences of trying to maintain the external value of a currency 'artificially' once the country's international competitiveness had been undermined.[100]

Moreover, there were attractive instances of devaluations being 'successful' in the classical sense: for example, the devaluation of the pound in 1931. But those who would take this case as a basis for generalization (and they account for the majority of the neo-classical and even Keynesian schools) seem to forget (a) that in that year Britain was the most powerful import market in the world; (b) that, therefore, most of Britain's suppliers followed suit; (c) that Britain was suffering at the time from a savage deflation, with unemployment above 20 per cent; and (d) that Britain supplemented the devaluation by general tariff protection, while at the same time securing Imperial Preference in its most important export markets. This formidable (not to say abhorrent) array of conditions for the 'success' of the 1931 operation is sufficient to rule it out as an exemplar.

There was, also, the German resurgence after 1949–50 and, a little later, that of Japan. But these two vanquished nations were forced into an undervaluation of their currencies by the occupying Powers[101]—especially the United States—in an attempt to eradicate the 'inflationary' consequences of the war on their monetary and banking structures. And, finally, there was the example of France after the second devaluation of the 1957–8 period (the first devaluation having failed as a result of the Algerian war and rising costs).

In all these cases, however, there were good specific national reasons for success. In the case of Germany there was a traumatic fear that wage- and price-increases would lead to a renewed inflationary débâcle. In Japan, success was encouraged by the peculiar social structure and the paternalistic system of industrial relations. Indeed, in the defeated countries any political odium which might accrue from the brutality of devaluation could be transferred on to the occupying Powers.

In France and Germany, moreover, the principal reason for the success of these measures is most probably the negligible bargaining power on the side of labour: in the former as a result of the failure of the General Strike and of the absorption of the Algerian French and the peasantry leaving the land; and in Germany as a result of the massive immigration, first of Germans from Eastern and South-eastern Europe (and subsequently from its own agricultural sector), and afterwards of 'guest' labour from the less developed countries of Southern Europe. The gains were immense. Japan and Italy too had large reserves of non-industrial labour to tap. Exports increased and the rise in profits stimulated investment and productivity; in turn the rate of increase in real wages was accelerated. The 'miracle' of a virtuous circle became established.

The maintenance of an export surplus as a result of the undervaluation of a currency has, of course, great socio-political attractions. To German public opinion its appeal was particularly striking. Germany's position as a persistent creditor in recent years, for instance, seemed to present an admirable means of regaining its lost strength and prestige after the war. A country cannot for ever incur deficits, because its creditors will not lend to it indefinitely. On the other hand, surpluses can be maintained indefinitely, on the basis of which a country can extend or refuse credits to its industrialized debtors (and aid to developing countries) at will. It follows that a persistent creditor can behave like a Great Power—and this is exactly what German ministers were able to do in the autumn of 1968. It is hardly an advantage to be given up lightly.

Undervaluation can also bring with it considerable domestic advantages, especially for a Conservative government, since the running of a substantial surplus permits the maintenance of full employment and capacity production without the need for corresponding proportionate increases in internal demand. Profits can increase as a proportion of national income without hindering the expansion of demand, while the unrestricted capacity to export will permit the adoption of more efficient production methods through the exploitation of economies of scale. The rapid growth of exports then stimulates a continuing increase in the rate of productivity growth. This in turn further tends to increase competitiveness, provided that the relative rate of increase in wage costs per unit of output remains low. The fact that *real* wages are increasing at a faster rate—despite a distribution of income which is less favourable to wage-earners than in more sluggish economies such as Britain or even the United States—reduces the opposition of trade unions to such a policy. Although the direct effect of revaluation would amount to an increase in the real purchasing-power of the lower income groups, and in consumption generally, indirectly the decrease in Germany's competitiveness in foreign markets might react on investment and thus weaken the mechanism of growth in real income.

These considerations are a formidable deterrent against 'progressive' policies and help to explain the hostility of a wide section of the German population, at the time of the Bonn conference in the autumn of 1968, to suggestions by the United States and Britain that the Mark should be revalued. Indeed the Social Democrats later took a considerable risk in advocating and pushing through a revaluation (by means of floating) of the Mark in September 1969 immediately before the election. No other country (except perhaps Japan) could have succeeded in this so decisively.

The fate of the Socialist-led Coalition in Germany hung on whether the country's international competitive strength rested on deep-seated social factors, or whether it was thought that the revaluation would lead to a cut in investment, and on whether any eventual slack would be taken up by an expansion of domestic demand. If the effects of revaluation were to have been aggravated by a burst of successful wage demands, and if this resulted in the formation of unfavourable longer-term expectations and a decline in investment, then the outlook for the Coalition would have been bleak indeed.[102] Fortunately, and against all expectations, things did not turn out that way.

The basic imbalance between the leading countries is the result of the divergence in the movement of costs and partly of capital movements which are either not justified by the availability of resources or are of a speculative nature. This in turn is partly a reflection of differences in historical background and rates of economic growth. The reluctance of creditor countries to shoulder some of the burden of readjustment by expanding domestic demand is to some extent rooted in their indignation at being expected to 'import inflation' from countries whose rate of cost 'creep' is faster than their own, and possibly faster than is politically acceptable to them. This intractability is clearly a serious obstacle to such an adjustment mechanism where rates of inflation diverge considerably.

None the less it is the case that revaluation can help to keep inflation in check and to restore international balance. In particular, revaluations are likely to be free of those drawbacks which render devaluations so risky. If devaluation leads to compensatory wage- and price-increases, the intended improvement in the country's competitive position will be cancelled. This will probably provoke (renewed) attacks on its currency, hence making a further devaluation inevitable. In contrast, it is virtually inconceivable that the equilibrating effects of a revaluation will be offset by compensatory reductions in wages and costs. This crucial asymmetry between devaluation and revaluation is of the first importance in any discussion of exchange-rate policy, to which we now turn.

(c) *Exchange rates, inflation and equilibrium*

The discussion of the relationship between exchange-rate policy and the internal economic situation of a country has been conducted conventionally in terms which preclude analysis of the concomitant relationship of exchange rates with inflation. This should come as no surprise—despite the fact that the matter was thrashed out at the time of the 'Bretton Woods' crisis of 1947.[103] In the years since 1945 a great number of devaluations have occurred, some of which, particularly in Germany and Japan, have helped in securing substantial export surpluses. Yet the official attitude has always been hostile to devaluation. Even though Keynes claimed that the Bretton Woods arrangements were the very antithesis of a gold standard, inasmuch as they permitted parity changes and provided for the creation of additional (albeit borrowed) reserves, nevertheless changes in parities (i.e. those in excess of 10 per cent) were hedged about with conditions. In particular, they were made contingent upon the Fund being convinced that the country in question was in 'fundamental disequilibrium'—that is, that a deficit in the balance of payments persisted at 'acceptable' levels of unemployment. However enlightened this proviso was in offering a compromise between stubborn resistance and the competitive debauching of currencies, by implication it condemned those responsible for the monetary and economic management which gave rise to such fundamental disequilibria. In fact a great many governments failed to survive devaluations. As a consequence it could be assumed by all and sundry that governments would, within (and even beyond) tolerable limits, strive to maintain the existing parity of their currencies.

Under such conditions a *pattern of anticipations* came to characterize markets whereby devaluations would not be used as an everyday means of national economic management. This had the effect of precluding the irruption of expectations of cumulative interactions between the foreign and domestic values of any currency. In other words, it could be (and was) assumed that a devaluation would not accelerate the rate of increase in wage and other income demands. So long as an anti-devaluation sentiment prevailed this would not in general have been an unwarranted assumption. No doubt some price increases would be inevitable, mainly as a result of increases in import- and export-prices in terms of the domestic currency; but this, after all, is the way in which adjustment is intended to work. It would have been expected, however, that these increases would be kept within bounds and not multiplied by anticipatory or autonomous increases in incomes. It is solely in such a context and against such an historical background, however, that it is plausible to assume that domestic costs and prices would be only loosely connected with the rate of exchange, and that the direct and immediate effects of a change in that rate would not be swamped by the indirect and potentially more substantial impact of cumulative inflationary anticipations. Such expectations, however, must be discarded as soon as a conscious policy of exchange-rate adjustment, whether once-for-all, 'crawling' or completely flexible, is accepted as one of the 'regular' instruments of currency or balance-of-payments management.

We have already alluded to the dangers inherent in such a 'positive' approach to exchange-rate policy as lying in the fundamentally asymmetrical response of domestic incomes with respect to changes in the external and internal values of the currency. Revaluation, on the one hand, may reasonably be expected to succeed in restoring balance, since its effect on real incomes is unlikely to be offset by any fall in money wages as import prices fall. For this reason it is also improbable that any general anticipatory movements will ensue in the expectation of further upward changes in the parity. The Rey Report,[104] as well as the proposals put forward by the I.M.F.[105] and by the United States Secretary of the Treasury,[106] are all recent examples of how this asymmetry is still disregarded in official circles; moreover, the devaluation-bias against the dollar might well be replaced under the proposed new system by an even worse deflation-bias, thus risking a return to the 1955–7 recession and currency troubles.

On the other hand, the effects of a devaluation, as we have emphasized, might easily be nullified by protective compensatory wage demands which, if met, would unleash an accelerated vicious circle of further inflation and depreciation. Yet this contingency has been consistently and stubbornly neglected, not least by Keynesians.

Implicitly the approach adopted to the problem of international economic relations has been either that of the classical Keynesian income-determination framework, or that of the monetarist Quantity Theory, extended to include foreign trade. Neither has in fact shown itself fit to account for the actual course of events. Monetarists in particular have been so confident of the efficacy of their proposed policy of 'secular' monetary expansion as to have been initially in favour of nothing less than completely freely floating exchange rates. Now, however, an extraordinary new twist has been given to the monetarist controversy: it now seems that exchange rates are 'irrelevant'. According to Professor Parkin the monetarists have lately 'proven'—at least to his own satisfaction—that devaluations are exactly offset by an acceleration in the rate of inflation, the latter in turn being determined by the rate of domestic credit expansion (whatever that may mean). Thus: '*differential rates of domestic credit expansion are the cause of both exchange-rate adjustments and differential inflation rates*';[107] and since '*exchange rates are largely irrelevant* ... the key thing a country, when in deficit, has to do to re-establish external equilibrium is to cut domestic credit expansion'.[108] In other words, anticipations and monetary movements, hence prices and the balance of payments, are predictable because proportional to the amount of devaluation (or depreciation), without more ado. This is the opposite of the orthodox Keynesian fallacy, and surely just as dangerous.

Professor Parkin's assertions, however, are not supported by any data, but simply by references to (as yet) unpublished articles. This is a practice which has become increasingly widespread since he and Professor Lipsey adopted it to impress people with their 'proof' that incomes policy is counter-productive and detrimental to stability, and presumably on the basis of similar statistical techniques.[109] When that 'proof' was published, however, it was dealt with by myself and Mr. L. Godfrey.[110] (It would be useful if some consultation were to take place between economists and logicians on the question as to what constitutes proof and how far regression analysis can establish causal nexus.)

In effect, however, discussion of exchange-rate policy still centres on the question as to how far the incorrect valuation of a currency tends (a) to distort the disposition of resources from their 'optimal' allocation and (b) to reduce the efficacy of interest-rate policy. The response of capital movements, especially to fluctuations in exchange rates, is assumed to be 'normal', that is to say, a fall in the rate would discourage rather than stimulate further outflows. Thus the liberalization of capital movements since the war, which were in fact destabilizing, has been consistently treated as a means of achieving stability, to be promoted by the adjustment of capital flows in response to international differences in interest rates.[111] Moreover, proponents of gradual parity changes see interest-rate differentials as the most effective means of offsetting anticipations of cumulative exchange-rate movements. Their opponents, however, stress the fear that speculative flows may not be so easily abated, no matter how gentle the initiating change, since they may gather momentum as a result of hopes of future capital gain. In these circumstances manageable changes in interest rates may be far from adequate in reversing such flows.

This traditional approach to the question of exchange-rate policy has been strengthened by the conventional view that the causes of international disequilibria are typically attributable to fiscal irresponsibility stemming from hostility to—and consequent weakness of—economic 'discipline'. This in turn is seen as being a common failing of democratic régimes. Countries are seen to 'get into a position' requiring readjustment because of miscalculations as to the extent to which they can 'get away with' inflation. This attitude sounds curiously old-fashioned. It is, perhaps, a survival from European experience immediately after World War I; no doubt the record of certain less developed countries such as Indonesia and in Latin America has something to do with it also. As such, however, it has very little to do with the problem of the highly industrialized countries of the West since World War II.[112]

There has been a firm disregard, furthermore, of the impact-effect of parity changes on competing countries. Now the reallocation of resources implies investment, or at least reinvestment, and a movement in exchange rates has identical effects on competitors as does the imposition of tax-cum-subsidies (so abhorred by those in favour of the former). In an atmosphere where parities are not guaranteed, estimates of future profitability become additionally hazardous. In a situation, moreover, where the currency of a developed country has come under attack—however justified the belief that it has become overvalued—devaluation might not only fail to cure the international payments imbalance, it might also add fuel to the fire (although the devaluation of the currency of a small primary-producing country would not meet with these perils). Devaluation inevitably increases a country's import bill. On the other hand, the total foreign-exchange value of its exports may not rise for some time, that is, until the new prices can be embodied in new orders and/or the volume of exports rises sufficiently. Should this delay give rise to renewed anticipations, a cumulative movement might well ensue, leading to a further and possibly more dangerous attack on the currency.

Such a pattern of events would seem to have accounted for the 'failure' of the 'devaluation' of the dollar in December 1971 to reverse the export of short-term capital from the United States. In the case of the dollar, other central banks intervened to prevent its further depreciation. Thus, according to Mr. Peter Jay:

It was accepted that during the 18 months or two years before the revaluation of currencies had worked through to correct the United States deficit, other countries would have to take further dollars into their reserves. Everybody seemed willing to do this on the basis of what has come to be known as the 'J-shape' movement of a country's balance of payments after a devaluation. . . . The behaviour of foreign exchange markets in recent weeks is ascribed in part to the failure of private operators to understand the 'J-shape', although there is some suspicion that finance ministers themselves left Washington without fully appreciating or preparing for the phenomenon themselves.[113]

A similar conjuncture to this (including delayed deflationary action which, in this case, was more perilous) was to be observed in Britain in 1968. Thus, having demonstrated the remarkably low (in some cases perverse) price-elasticities characterizing British trade (as compared with what had been believed at the time of devaluation), the research staff of the National Institute concluded:

Moreover, one should not lose sight of the fact that the transition from devaluation to the 'ultimate effect' is not direct. Export earnings in terms of foreign currency fall to begin with and only start to increase again when the rise in the volume of exports offsets the effect of this fall. In the British case in 1967 there was a net loss in foreign earnings in the first year, which was just offset by the increased earnings in the second year, so that there is a sense in which for exports of manufactures devaluation did not begin to work until after nearly two years.[114]

Should adverse anticipations lead to a renewed and successful speculative attack on a recently devalued currency, and if the resulting increase in domestic prices spark off further wage demands (for the reasons mentioned above), a downward spiral in the external and internal values of the currency will be virtually unavoidable unless drastic deflationary steps are taken. But this, as we have seen, can only work if attended by (or if it elicits) a reversal in psychological attitudes, and that demands a policy of 'overkill', in other words, mass unemployment. These considerations show how misconceived and gravely misleading is the anodyne injunction of the so-called High Level Group in its Report to the Secretary-General of O.E.C.D. that 'measures to influence the domestic economy should be used to re-establish external balance in all cases where they can be made effective without leading a deficit country to serious and lasting unemployment or a surplus country to serious inflation'.[115] Pangloss could hardly have bettered it.

The failure of the orthodox Keynesian demand-management approach to stabilization has been attributed to an unwarranted adherence to fixed exchange rates. Yet neither Keynesian nor liberal–conservative monetarists advocates of the 'free' price- or market-mechanism have considered the implications of their arguments for the problem of anticipatory speculation.

In the absence of some purposive policy to hold down persistent cost movements in debtor countries, monetary gadgets such as crawling pegs or widening bands cannot fulfil their claim to providing the elements of an easy yet stable solution. To this question we shall devote somewhat greater attention in the final chapter.

4. The Elements of a Solution

THE brunt of the argument so far has been that orthodox global methods of maintaining international balance have failed. They have failed for the reason that they have been based on the fallacious assumption that international trade is conducted by atomistically organized units in a framework of perfect competition, and is characterized by sub-units alternately expanding and contracting by means of which the system as a whole is kept in overall balance.

In fact international economic relations have become typically oligopolistic, and that in two senses at least. In the first place, *national* policies—whether monetary, fiscal, or exchange-rate policy, or the impact of more direct policy weapons such as incomes policy (freeze) or diverse controls and discriminatory subsidies—will affect, if not all, then at least a large number of firms actually trading within the country in which action is taken. Thus, the simple, direct, signals of the market to these units which cannot be affected by any single one of them are superseded, or at least very strongly modified, by the actions of (significant) members of the world economic trading system. Thus, most important trading nations must needs formulate policy in the light of policies followed by other important trading nations and on an assessment of how these in turn are themselves likely to react. (Even in the period when gold movements were quasi-automatically linked with changes in the policies of central banks and Treasuries, the primacy, if not dominance, of Britain was apparent.) The relative national strength (based on size, productivity and degree of self-sufficiency), and the policies (including reserve-holding) that the dominant countries pursue, play an overwhelmingly important part in setting the tone and determine the outcome. The old Humean mechanism is no longer a realistic image of the behaviour of world trade and payments.

In the second place, there is the increasing prominence of large, multi-national firms—necessarily few in number—both domestically and, increasingly so, internationally. While these are open to direct pressure from strong countries, they are themselves capable of exerting pressure on weak countries. Their trading policies are not entirely, or even predominantly, motivated by the instantaneous maximization of profits in the short run. This factor profoundly alters the nature of international trade, payments and capital movements in a sense wholly ignored by conventional economics. The persistent failure to deal with the problem of cost inflation, which inevitably entails the same failure to analyse most international disturbances, is clearly a direct consequence of this refusal to accept the unalterable.

Nothing illustrates this more strikingly than the profound change which has overtaken the world monetary system. The position after 1947—that is, after the breakdown of the original concept of Bretton Woods and the initiation of Marshall Aid—was characterized by a rapid expansion in world trade and by a virtually uninterrupted increase in production. This expansion was, however, periodically slowed down when the rise in prices—also uninterrupted (in sharp contrast with the period before 1914)—seemed politically intolerable. As we have seen, the rate of inflation *and* reactions to restrictive policies have both been determined by institutional and historical factors. On the whole, however, a slowing down of expansion in any one industrial country 'worked', that is, in the sense of being sufficient to restore the balance of payments. No doubt the underlying trend in unemployment was upward, but it was a fraction of the rate prevailing between the wars. At the same time, however, the peripheral primary-producing countries suffered in this process from a deterioration in their terms of trade, both as a result of increasing money costs in industrial countries and as a result of falling primary-commodity prices whenever the latter applied restrictive policies.

This state of affairs, however, has been changing, at first gradually, and more recently at an increasing rate. We have been witnessing a reversion towards recurrent currency crises and, worse, the possibility of a return to the pre-war pattern of more widespread unemployment of productive capacity and manpower, and of threats of beggar-my-neighbour policies. Such retrogression can be halted only if its causes are correctly analysed and understood.

Until the mid-1960s the oligopolistic game had been dominated by the creditor countries—first principally the United States, and subsequently Germany. Other governments either could not afford, or were not prepared, to tolerate more than a limited degree of price inflation and balance-of-payments deficits of more than a certain size. The burden of readjustment was therefore placed upon debtor countries. Since devaluation or depreciation are in the first instance less painful than deflation, creditor countries tended as a matter of 'disciplinary' principle to resist the former as a means of adjustment for debtors, despite the fact that for terms-of-trade reasons the extent of the readjustment and deflation required to 'free' resources might be even greater. The comparative degree of deflation needed therefore depends on a host of factors.[1] In any case, imbalances were then still entirely identified with excess-demand pressures, which were fought primarily, if not exclusively, by restrictive monetary, or possibly budgetary, policies. Conversely, creditor countries were still satisfied with their surpluses and—with the exception of Germany and the Netherlands—did not revalue their currencies. The drift towards undervaluation was a *drift* and not the consequence of willed devaluation.

Since then, however, the picture has been increasingly overshadowed by the relentless increase in America's overall balance-of-payments deficit and the withering away of her current-account surplus. Resistance against 'imported' inflation sharpened. Unlike the British, however, the Americans, as we have seen, rapidly altered their stance and, using their bargaining power as a debtor country, threatened periodically to suspend convertibility—a threat which, after three years of bluff and counter-bluff, was ultimately carried out in 1971. Meanwhile, the menace of American competitiveness was forcing the European countries and, even more so, Japan to support the dollar by purchasing it in vast quantities in an attempt to forestall its depreciation.

Governed as the central banks are by bankers, no one seemed to detect anything anomalous in a situation in which hot money was being lent and re-lent in the Eurodollar market: it brought in revenue both for central and private banks. The inevitable result, however, was that a bear position could be built up against the dollar beyond all imagination. It was naïve in the extreme in such circumstances to suppose that a deluge of the suspect currency would not flood the strong currencies' markets in order to secure a quick capital gain by enforcing a revaluation, while the forces liberated by the speculative attack and the crisis of confidence would justify *ex post facto* the move by adding to the impetus of inflation. This connection between internal and external stability (or rather instability) paralyses the balancing mechanism of the system. Changes in parity may well be needed. In certain psychological conditions they may help in restoring balance in international payments. It is clear, however, that the interaction between devaluation or downward floating and inflation must be taken into account.[2] Indeed, if the experience of the last half-decade or so teaches anything it is that the secondary effects of general policy measures— whether devaluation or depreciation, as well as fiscal policy—might be far more important than the immediate, primary, direct effects. (We have seen more than one Chancellor or Minister of Finance worsted in his efforts to try to enforce contraction or expansion, only to have savings move in the wrong direction, thus overwhelming his 'finely tuned' measures.) This importance of secondary effects is much the greater in the case of a downward move in the rate of exchange where the country concerned has been suffering from inflation and weakness in its balance of payments. No doubt *any* measure to restore balance-of-payments equilibrium must have deflationary implications (unless there is widespread unemployment), as, indeed, has the *revaluation* of a creditor country's currency for that of debtor countries. The great difference is that the devaluation of a debtor country's currency has a general impact and is thus more likely to lead to secondary anticipatory reactions (and so to the need for further devaluation) than the discriminating increase in the price of the exports of a creditor country that has revalued *its* currency. The asymmetrical, internal differences between upward and downward movements in exchange rates have already been discussed.

A review of historical experience indicates that any future scheme, if it is to be viable and inherently stabilizing, must embody certain rules of conduct and sanctions. These rules in turn should be complemented by provisions for the creation of international liquidity, which must be sufficiently elastic, not only to respond to the needs of the world's current-account transactions, but also to help in the liquidation of what remains of the key-currency (dollar and sterling) exchange standard and to deal with possible crises of confidence.

Most recently, experience since 15 August 1971—and especially since the Smithsonian agreement—points the obvious moral that monetary reforms or measures alone cannot provide a satisfactory basis for steady expansion in the future. In particular, the agenda adopted for discussion in the communiqué of the Group of Ten in December 1971[3] was inadequate: similarly with the points listed by Mr. George Shultz,[4] which will presumably form the basis for discussion in the expanded Committee of Twenty. These still assume that monetary measures and arrangements (possibly reinforced by fiscal means) are sufficient to restore and maintain equilibrium.

We shall, therefore, deal first with the problem of rules of good conduct, agreement and adherence to which can alone prevent a repetition of the crises of the last two or three years. It is on this essential point that both our analysis and proposals differ from those of the monetarist and semi-monetarist schools.

1. RULES OF GOOD CONDUCT

The relationship between the major industrial countries being one of oligopoly, there will be a considerable pressure on individual countries to trim their economic policies according to those of other more important countries. So long as international reserves are relatively scarce, policies that are likely to boost reserves (i.e. restrictive policies) will tend to find favour—subject to their internal political consequences (*vide* Germany in 1966, France in 1968, the United States in 1971 or Britain in 1971–2); but countries which, as a direct consequence, find themselves to be losing reserves will soon be constrained to follow suit with restrictive policies of their own. Thus the (presumed) scarcity of reserves is likely to become exacerbated.

Secondly, the greater the differences among countries in their institutions and in their policies affecting relative cost levels and the balance of payments, the greater will be the need for reserves. The stronger and more active a country's trade unions, for instance, the more reserves it will require in order to gain time for relatively slow and less painful adjustments and to diminish the likelihood of retaliation abroad. This is particularly so if countries are prohibited by international agreement (from dealing with their foreign-exchange problems (at least temporarily) by direct means, such as surcharges, quota-regulations, export incentives and payments controls.

Thirdly, the development of an international market for liquid funds, such as the Eurodollar market, will again increase the need for reserves in order to avert the foreign-exchange crises (very often fostered by quite irrational fears, viz. that of Britain in 1957 and 1968, and of the United States in 1972), in anticipation of which vast sums of hot money are liable to flow from one country to another, and which just such markets are designed to facilitate. If suitable institutions are available—such as *banques d'affaires* or merchant banks—there will be a great temptation to use short-term funds, at relatively low rates of interest, for long-term purposes. Should any of these turn out to have been misplaced, the acute danger might arise of a general liquidation resulting in a collapse of the value of securities underlying the longer-term loans. This is precisely what happened in 1931–3. Destructive capital flights follow, culminating in a general crisis of liquidity.

It is such considerations that point to the desirability of rules of conduct that might minimize or limit the need for additional international liquidity. To this end concerted action by both (potential) creditor and debtor countries is needed on a number of fronts with a view to: (i) mitigating inflationary pressure so as to keep differences in cost and price increases within tolerable limits, especially in habitually 'debtor' countries (in other words, the discrepancy in the rate of inflation between important countries must be kept within certain narrow limits); (ii) permitting the maintenance of high levels of employment; (iii) stimulating as much as possible the economic growth of the less developed countries; and, above all, (iv) such concerted action should be designed to minimize the risk of aggravating the underlying causes of recent imbalances which, as we have seen, lies mainly in differential rates of inflation.

(i) Much the most important aim here is some kind of policy which will effectively limit inflation in (potential) debtor countries to a rate that would prove acceptable to creditor countries, that is, such that it might prove possible to achieve a balance in international payments without requiring creditor countries to accelerate their internal rates of inflation to a degree that they would consider (politically) intolerable. In particular, such a policy must ensure that, within narrow limits, anticipatory action on the part of either side of industry (including the service sector, and especially the professions) will not worsen the malaise. Recent experience, as analysed earlier in this essay, has shown that it is cost inflation rather than demand inflation that must be warded off and it is for this reason that prices and incomes (rather than fiscal or monetary) policy is called for. Should demand inflation manifest itself, however, then deflationary measures will have to be implemented in the debtor country concerned. If, on the other hand, imbalances arise as a result of the underemployment of resources in a leading country, then reflationary measures must be enforced. We shall be discussing the possible counterparts of these policies on the monetary plane.

(ii) In the first instance, temporary surcharges or quotas might be superior (or at least less risky) as a means of readjustment, since they are more easily reversed than changes in exchange rates.

(iii) In cases where resources are, or threaten to become, underemployed, the above courses of action might be supplemented by measures aimed at the purposive creation of demand for the products of the industrially developed debtor countries. Plans for such a scheme were elaborated during the war,[5] based on the consideration that aggregate demand would have to be stimulated on a world-wide basis if a powerful group of creditor countries happened to be suffering from unemployment. Such an increase in demand could be effected, for instance, by granting to the less developed countries an allocation of S.D.R.s in excess of their normal quotas, which would be expendable in the developed debtor countries (the normal quotas themselves could be increased in some inverse proportion to national income, thus establishing a firm 'link' between S.D.R.s and development grants). Of course, this type of arrangement would only be feasible if the industrialized countries, while benefiting from these proposed increases in liquidity, agreed to embark on programmes of readjustment.

(iv) It is essential that a collective system of supervision be developed which would take due account of these difficult analytical problems and which would strive to avoid any action which might exacerbate imbalances either in a deflationary or inflationary direction.

2. FLEXIBILITY

The importance of eliminating persistent tendencies toward balance-of-payments surpluses or deficits, then, is overriding. But oligopoly is not only a feature of international relations, it is also a domestic phenomenon. That is to say, internally we live in a non-Keynesian micro-oligopolistic world, in which wage demands can be shifted on to managed (domestic) prices. Relatively speaking the old macro-economic beggar-my-neighbour struggle for export surpluses between the industrialized countries (in the sense of countries trying to achieve export-led growth on the basis of surpluses resulting from deliberately undervalued currencies, or by drifting into this position as a result of productivity increases not being reflected in wages) in the interests of increasing or maintaining employment has become far less important as trade unions all over the world (including even the Communist bloc) attain increases in money wages out of line with productivity growth. If a country's currency becomes 'undervalued' it is a sign that efficiency wages in that country, relative to its import-competing and export capacity, have been increasing at a slower rate than elsewhere. Thus, the likelihood is that, after devaluing, the basic imbalance will again emerge in time. *Once-for-all* adjustments to parities alone cannot eradicate the continuous tendency for cost structures as between countries with different institutional arrangements and historical backgrounds to diverge. But the alternative (of repeated or continuous parity changes) may be equally unable to deal with this problem, because they will tend to induce an intensification of the inflation-depreciation spiral, thus robbing the parity change of its rationale. Such a course, therefore, would be fraught with dangers.

All experience suggests that we are here confronted with a crucial asymmetry in the functioning of the modern economic system which has been and continues to be disregarded by both neo-orthodox schools of economics: an upward revision of an exchange-parity does not have the mirror-image consequences of an equivalent downward adjustment.

(a) Downward flexibility

If the basic reason for imbalance lies in a persistent pattern of cost divergencies the most likely contingency is that the 'weak' or 'soft' currencies will experience a continuous fall in the value of money in terms of goods and services and foreign currency. Moreover, the effects of this would be exaggerated under a régime of floating rates. In this respect the attitude of the advocates of floating rates indicates the extent to which economic theorizing is dominated by events in the (often very) recent past. Bretton Woods banished the fear of uncontrolled competitive devaluations, even of frequent parity changes. This had been a reaction against the then vivid memory of the critical monetary developments which had bedevilled much of the 1920s and 1930s. But *now* the disadvantage of exchange stability in the context of divergent cost movements has become such an obsessive preoccupation that the implications of exchange instability—as a result of those very divergencies—for *internal* costs and prices are in turn neglected. As we have seen, the danger that a downward revision or floating of an exchange rate would provoke wage demands is highly acute, while it is less likely that an upward revision or float would lead to a fall in the rate of increase in wages.

(b) *Upward flexibility*

Very different would be the impact of a greater degree of upward flexibility in 'strong' currencies. But since the equilibrating effects of revaluation are unlikely to be undone by compensating domestic income adjustments, for political reasons it is likely to meet with severe opposition (*vide* Germany and Japan). Furthermore, it seems that the efficacy of upward adjustment, even within political limits, is not as great as might have been hoped. The 'elasticity optimists', apart from pursuing a wholly unsound methodology, have been shown to be ridiculously unsound also in their quantitative claims.[6] We have already argued (in the introduction to this chapter), however, that revaluation is likely to be more selective, less pervasive and therefore psychologically less dangerous in its impact-effects than devaluation.

(c) *Crawling*

The crawling peg is an ingenious attempt at compromise. Yet again if relative costs tend to creep only in one direction—as is implicit in the operation of the device—the same problem will re-emerge, as happened in the wake of the German revaluation in 1961. Ultimately the fear of persistent depreciation will wreck the system, since everybody will want to get out of the weak currencies in expectation of their continuous decline. Without having first eliminated the disparity in cost trends the basic problem would be exacerbated rather than cured. It is argued that the maintenance of international differentials in interest rates in favour of the downward-sliding currencies (i.e. equivalent to the divergence in the cost creep) would be sufficient to restore equilibrium. If the cost differential is within the agreed limits of the exchange-rate crawl, and if its persistence does not lead to its acceleration as a result of anticipations on the part of trade unions and employers, then such an argument would be valid. But in the context of the struggle between the two sides of industry such stability in the rate of depreciation is most unlikely.[7]

If, due to domestic inflation, the decline in the internal value of money accelerates, the rate of decline in the exchange rate will itself lose credibility —much as the credibility of fixed parities was lost—since everybody will fear an increase in the rate of depreciation, hence unleashing a speculative attack against the suspect currency. Indeed, because of the 'legitimacy' of the downward crawl, the force of the speculation might be the more intense than in the case of a fixed rate of exchange. People will begin to suspect that the real value of their money assets and savings was being endangered. The domestic political consequences of a quickened depreciation, moreover, might be incalculable; the example of Germany in 1922–4 and 1945–8 should open the eyes of those who conduct economic arguments in a political vacuum.

Alternatively a continuous upward crawl in the exchange rate of a 'strong' currency—of (say) 2 per cent per annum—might have certain beneficial effects, for the reason that the speculative urge abroad to exploit its appreciation would tend to be restrained by its very unimpressiveness, while the asymmetry in the behaviour of wage movements (in the sense that they would not fall) would represent a disequilibrating speculative movement. But if the efficacy of the exchange-rate crawl is unimpressive in terms of minimizing speculative gains, it will be equally unimpressive in its effects in curing a persistent balance-of-payments surplus.

(d) *Widening band*

Yet another attempt at compromise—first adumbrated by Keynes in 1923 with respect to the buying and selling price of gold[8]—consists in retaining fixed exchange rates, but with wider margins between the intervention points on either side of official parities. Indeed, this is precisely what happened in the aftermath of the 1971–2 dollar crisis, when it was agreed that margins should be extended from 1 to $2\frac{1}{4}$ per cent on either side of the new so-called central rates against the dollar. Since the rate between any two *non-dollar* currencies can fluctuate by as much as double the spread permitted individually for any currency *vis-à-vis* the dollar, that is, if one happens to be at its ceiling and the other at its floor, the result of the wider margins is to allow in principle for mutual depreciations (appreciations) among non-dollar currencies of up to 9 per cent, compared with the earlier maximum of 4 per cent.

From the point of view of helping to bring about basic readjustments, the degree of fluctuation presently permitted is well within normal profit margins. Hence, even in respect of a country whose currency is bumping along its permissible floor or ceiling, it is hardly likely that the 'real' structural changes required to effect the basic balance of payments will occur— although it would certainly have imperilled the Common Market's 'uniform price' system, which explains the French opposition to widened bands and their insistence on a narrowing of intervention points *within* the Community.[9] The risk of further unfavourable (downward) moves in the exchange rate will be appreciable in its effect on *new* fixed investment, although it is not impossible that some stimulus might be given to import-replacing investment and to the export of commodities produced with existing equipment. But if a currency continues to bob along at its lower limit for any length of time, with its basic position patently deteriorating, it is more than likely to come under attack, particularly so if it is seen that the situation is not being 'cured' thereby. Perhaps the only advantage of wider bands is that they afford some check on 'normal' capital movements because of the added risk involved. As a result, capital markets might become more isolated, thus permitting a widening of international interest-rate differentials. For those who, like myself, believe in the greater likelihood of capital movements being unbalancing than the reverse, this is certainly an advantage.

It is fairly evident from these considerations that the problem of restoring and maintaining international balance will not be solved by making concessions in the direction of 'flexibility'; depreciation by debtor countries presages a slippery path to disaster, while appreciation by creditors is unlikely to be a politically feasible alternative in the long run.

The maintenance of balance in the world economy in the long run depends, in my opinion, on the use of more direct means of intervention. This does *not* mean that parities should be sacrosanct. If, in the longer run, structural changes in world production patterns or 'technical progress' result in the collapse of the market for certain goods (or goods produced by traditional methods); if internal political struggles lead to violent changes in costs; or if full employment is threatened by a severe slump abroad—then a change in the parity may be a valuable, indeed indispensable part of a policy package. But devaluation, if it is to 'work', must remain an exceptional and relatively rare measure. If not, repetitions will be anticipated (correctly so in any of the proposed flexible systems) and the device will destroy itself as an effective instrument of policy, and with it the stability of the societies that rely on it. In other words, the success of parity changes depends on a high degree of 'money illusion', on forgetfulness.

Clearly, resort to exchange-rate manipulation is no substitute for a deliberate policy aimed at eliminating the basic cause of international imbalances, or at least restricting imbalances to tolerable limits; this in turn must involve effective measures to keep price (and cost) increases in *debtor* countries to within a range (probably less than 3 per cent per annum) which would itself be acceptable to (currently) persistent creditor countries. And this one cannot expect to achieve by fiscal or monetary policies alone (whether or not supplemented by exchange-rate adjustments), which, as we have seen, are quite inadequate or involve unacceptable levels of unemployment.

Towards the end of 1969 I wrote:

> The conclusion is inevitable that both the UK and the US will be driven towards incomes or 'guide-post' policy. In default of such a policy the pattern of cost and price development may have grave political consequences either through a persistent inflation of prices leading to speculative attacks on the currency, or through unemployment. The regular alternating sequence of this cycle is the one stable feature of the post-war history of both countries.

A deliberate return to incomes policy would be much facilitated if an acceleration in the rate of increase in productivity could be achieved. Given the expectations for increases in money incomes, the higher is the rate of the increase in productivity the less is the inflation.

Unfortunately it is hardly to be expected that a rational solution will prove acceptable without a crisis giving a sharper edge to an obvious need. This applies as much to the creditor countries' aversion to expansion for fear of inflation and to handing over power to an international agency, as to the debtors' resistance to incomes policy. Yet without heavier unemployment only an incomes policy can assure a harmonization of the policies of countries whose socio-economic structures show sharp divergencies. It becomes more and more evident that it was the absence of such a conscious policy of harmonization which was at the bottom of the much sharper economic fluctuations and social distress before the Second World War. Are we going to revert to that pattern, presided over by Central Bankers? [The shift of real power towards this group is attested by the increasing importance of the Bank for International Settlements which in the early post-war years did little more than organize emergency aid in the form of swaps. Even the General Arrangements to Borrow seem unduly influenced by financial considerations. The relation of debtor governments to Central Bankers has reverted to the position of 1925–31.] The question is wide open.[10]

I have no reason to regret this prediction. It was made when the then new American President (Mr. Nixon), the British Chancellor of the Exchequer, and the Leader of the Opposition (soon to become Prime Minister) all gaily denigrated, triumphantly ridiculed and confidently forswore any kind of government intervention or influence in the sphere of money incomes. They were one and all defeated.

The degree of reliance on incomes and prices policy will, as we have seen, depend mainly on the social ambience in any one country; on the strength and militancy of its unions; on the latitude of the government's choice as between policy weapons; and on the political tolerance of unemployment. The more alienated the unions; the greater their strength; the more the government is restricted to using indirect, monetary and fiscal, measures; the less the tolerance of unemployment—the more necessary it is to rely on incomes policy. Unfortunately, the greater also will be the obstacles to its success. From this point of view Germany and Japan on the one hand, and the United States on the other, are, for different reasons, in a relatively favourable position—in contrast to Britain and, to a lesser extent, Italy.

The rise of regional combinations such as the Common Market has much complicated the problem, since they generally restrict their members' choice of policy weapons. Not only does membership of the E.E.C. render devaluation illegal, it makes it prohibitively expensive. As we have seen, the permissible range of fluctuation as between member countries' exchange rates is to be narrowed to zero. The capacity of member countries to pursue regional policies within their own borders is severely restricted. Therefore the degree of freedom permitted in these respects will be determined increasingly by the freedom required by more favourably situated countries such as Germany. The Germans, on the other hand, will be called upon to sustain the pound against non-E.E.C. currencies, while the French (who are mainly motivated by their attitude to the C.A.P., which is based on fixed exchange rates) will insist on keeping the ground rules, with little net cost to themselves. Thus Britain, which has so far been unable to solve its problems under far more favourable conditions, has burdened itself with artificial fetters and weights at a time when it is about to negotiate more perilous rapids.

We can only hope that the need for incomes policies in all major countries will be recognized and that the means will be found whereby to co-ordinate them in a way that will minimize the difficulties of maintaining international trade and payments in balance and not endanger the steady expansion of the leading countries of the world economy, that is, of the world economy itself.

3. CAPITAL MOVEMENTS

It is essential that the rules of good conduct should include some form of control over capital movements, both inward and outward. This precept had been accepted originally even at Bretton Woods. It would be intolerable for the Americans to be able to use their potentially overwhelming industrial strength to force other countries to allow their currencies to appreciate or the dollar to 'depreciate'—and hence face industrial attack from the United States—as the only alternative to accumulating idle dollar balances, the proceeds of which are used by American (or rather United States-based multi-national) companies to acquire industrial and exhaustible natural assets. (This danger has never been recognized in Britain, where acceptance of direct investment and inflows of hot money has always been complete. Indeed the practice has been for hot money to be attracted in order to repay stable borrowings from official—whether bilateral or multilateral— sources. Mr. Cecil King's Diary testifies eloquently to the incompetence and ignorance of the luminaries of the Bank of England. The French, for all their ardour in favour of the simplicity of a gold bullion standard, recognized the need for control over capital movements, while the Germans became unwilling converts only in 1972.) This vital point had been stressed by Keynes in the Bretton Woods preparatory talks and was one of the few features of the British plan to be incorporated into the Final Act. As we have seen, it has been completely abandoned by the Executive Directors of the Fund. The neo-orthodox schools insist on regarding capital movements as 'stabilizing' and assume that capital imports, especially direct investment, are beneficial to the host country. Under certain limiting assumptions—such as a shortage of entrepreneurial ability or technical competence—this may well be so.[11] Modern international economic systems are not based on full employment or 'real' values. More recently, such capital exports have served to import inflation into the host country at a heavy cost in terms of future burdens. Equally essential, therefore, would be the institution of some sort of multilateral control and strict limitation of the growth of foot-loose Eurocurrency markets, a task that is well beyond the capacity of any single central bank. The vagaries of these markets and the fluctuations of massive waves of hot short-term funds are a constant and constantly increasing threat to stability. Central banks should restrict their 're-cycling' activities to direct loans to fellow central banks.

Unfortunately the United States Administration now seem to be advocating the automatization of readjustment, that is, of parity changes or 'appropriate' (i.e. inflationary or deflationary) monetary and fiscal policy on the basis of *changes in a country's reserves*. Unless overall agreements can be arrived at as regards monetary movements and longer-term investment (especially in industrialized areas), acceptance of this proposal would amount to an intolerable burden on the trading partners of the United States. In any case the data on most countries are so deficient and often misleading that the imposition of such an automatic mode of adjustment might have intolerable effects. The most that one can advocate is a continuous surveillance of *all major* countries and monthly high-level meetings with special emphasis being placed on countries' *full-employment* current balances and official capital flows. Co-ordinated control over the latter must become as essential an item in policy decisions as the adjustment of the former. The *de facto* overall balance of payments is not an appropriate indicator. So far as the rest of the world is concerned, a similar surveillance should be directed at actual current-account movements.

As an alternative to direct controls on capital movements, France and Belgium have recently followed closely the example of certain Latin American countries, that is by allowing exchange rates to fluctuate freely on a separate 'capital' or 'financial' exchange market so as to deter unwarranted inflows. I do not share the horror felt by some at the consequential misallocation of resources,[12] since I have little hope that in a world of internal pricing by multi-national corporations 'optimal' allocation can be achieved by non-interference. My objection is based rather on the inefficiency of the controls, which may well result in extensive profiteering on the part of the largest of these corporations without preventing the alienation of important industries. In the absence of effective direct controls, however, a multiple exchange-rate system is certainly preferable to non-intervention.

4. SUPPLYING LIQUIDITY

According to our analysis of recent monetary developments and crises the need for international reserves will depend on:

(i) The aims and means of economic policy in the leading countries and, more especially, on whether the aims of their policies are compatible with one another;

(ii) the institutional differences between leading countries in the organization of their trade unions and employers' federations and in their attitude to wage negotiations, which in turn influence wage increases;

(iii) the quality of management and the allocation of resources for productive investment and, thus, on the real (non-monetary) factors governing productivity growth; and

(iv) the role played by international reserves in assuring harmony in the execution of policy, in relation to other, especially more direct, means.

The need for liquidity is a function *not of the volume of trade but of the size of the likely imbalances* in international payments. This in turn is determined by the policy framework prevailing in the dominant participating countries in the world trading system; this relates in particular to the range of admissible means of adjustment and the ends of policy, to the willingness and ability of countries to limit surpluses and deficits in international payments, and to the rapidity with which individual countries can, under the existing rules of the game, legitimately take steps to limit the consequences of imbalances, for instance by means of direct controls or flexible exchange rates (see Chapter 2 (3)).

(a) *The aims of reserve-creation*

A rational solution should provide for the strengthening of the International Monetary Fund (without necessitating a change of name) into a new *international central bank*. This organ would be empowered to create sufficient quantities of internationally acceptable means of payment—including reserves, *owned* and not borrowed—with the following ends in view:

(i) *The obviation of general deflationary pressure merely in consequence of the desire of surplus countries wishing to increase their reserves, while deficit countries strive to achieve surpluses.* On this score some predetermined criterion for the creation of reserves would be needed. This could be based on an index taking into account the volume and value of foreign trade, changes in real and money national income, and changes in national policies with respect to the handling of cost inflation on the one hand, and to reserve-holding on the other. If there is a tendency for the divergence in price movements as between the leading countries to widen and for prices in creditor countries or countries with more stable price levels to increase, the creation of international reserves should only be undertaken on condition that debtor (or less stable) countries agree to implement more direct readjustment measures, preferably some stringent action on incomes, rather than general deflationary measures which might overshoot the mark. Under these circumstances creditor countries may be required to revalue their currencies.

(ii) *The avoidance of general crises of confidence leading to the forced and cumulative devaluation of principal currencies.* Here it would be essential for the international agency to be empowered to act according to certain *ad hoc* discretionary powers; in particular, it would be necessary for it to have sufficient means for manoeuvre in order to stem cumulative liquidations in the Eurocurrency market, while promoting its control.

(iii) *The eventual consolidation or funding of the liabilities of the reserve-currency countries in exchange for the short-term liabilities of the I.M.F. or some other international financial conglomerate, such as the S.D.R. fund (administered by the I.M.F.).* The special debt of the reserve-currency countries would be automatically diminished as the new S.D.R.s are created and as they receive new allocations. In the meantime a low rate of interest might be charged. In order to obviate the relative shrinkage of the reserves of former reserve-currency countries, a new method of creating international reserves will have to be established.

(b) *The reform of present arrangements*

Present arrangements are evidently barely sufficient for (i), not sufficient for (ii) and far from adequate for (iii); only the suspension of the convertibility of the dollar into gold has paralysed the power of the persistent creditors to impose their own policy preferences on to the United States.

The ability to borrow from an international central bank would, of course, have the same effect as using the quotas of the Fund. It might be regarded as invidious and result in restrictive measures on the country in question. This would be perfectly justified at times when employment is high and discipline must be enforced to prevent a general demand inflation; it would not be sufficient, however, where there is a danger of cumulative deflation. If the powers of an international central bank were confined to 'rediscounting' there would be no reason for establishing one.

An effective international central bank, however, could undertake active open-market operations to increase liquidity in those countries which were legitimately in need of it. (The I.M.F. in fact inaugurated such international open-market operations by buying United States securities against gold.)

Such occasions would arise, for instance, when countries came under pressure because of a depression elsewhere. The problem will be to arrive at a satisfactory system of safeguards against maladministration and to establish an organization that will gain the confidence of both rich and poor, debtors and creditors, in which the best possible advice will have been secured before final decisions on policy are made.

5. THE 'LINK'

Ever since the question of monetary reforms was raised, both the less developed areas and people of good will in rich countries have tried to establish a 'link' between the creation of additional reserves and the supply of funds to those areas. The idea is very attractive: aid without tears. There would be no need for further tax increases to sustain development, either through bilateral or multilateral channels; there would be no direct bilateral relationship, while multilateral aid could be channelled through the most suitable agencies.

So long as the business cycle was characterized by cumulative upward and downward movements in prices and employment, reflecting respectively an excess or a deficiency in demand, such a (Keynesian) remedy would have been irresistible. All would gain: none would lose. Expansion (through simple reflation) and income equalization could be dealt with so to speak at one stroke. No doubt even then there might have been serious misgivings. If aid were used to any considerable extent as an anti-cyclical instrument, unwelcome cyclical fluctuations could be imparted to the developing areas which might be less able to ride the consequences of such periodic interruptions (even decline) in their development progress. Extremely skilful planning would be needed in order to intercalate the additional—cyclical—aid with the sustained or stable level of aid. In most cases this kind of expertise was not available to such countries.

Unfortunately, by the time that this type of intervention had found, if not general, then at least appreciable, acceptance, the antagonistic changes in the structure of the industrialized countries, the spread of oligopoly and the steady increase in the prominence of the problem of cost inflation, had increased the difficulties involved in managing international economic relations. Unemployment in the industrialized countries is almost universally the result of misguided and futile policies to contain cost inflation, and it is this too which is mainly responsible for the deterioration in the terms of trade facing the developing countries. This in turn means that more aid is required in order to maintain what has been a high—if perhaps not satisfactory[13]—rate of overall material progress (as contrasted with its distribution). A firm link between aid and the creation of liquidity would have to take account of the basic need for increased monetary circulation in the industrialized countries; it would be foolish to expect the poorer countries not to make use of the S.D.R.s put at their disposal, with an inevitable (if not precisely corresponding) increase in the demand for the exports of the developed countries that this will entail. Thus the link will have to be followed up by an arrangement[14] by which to channel part of the additional reserves towards the industrialized debtor countries, but which would simultaneously enforce an intensification of their process of readjustment.

All this means that the volume of what might be called 'unconditional link aid' must necessarily be limited and its channelling carefully planned. Additional 'extraordinary' link aid would be made available if the general world economic situation warranted it. The decision on this would be left to the discretion of a qualified majority on the Board of the I.M.F. In any case the distribution of additional reserves should be made dependent on the recipient country conforming with the minimum rules of good-neighbourly conduct. I do not believe that the poorer countries have a basic right to draw upon the richer without in their turn making at least a minimum effort to maintain conditions within their borders that are conducive to social progress. On both counts some important discretionary powers will have to reside with the I.M.F. or its successor institution.

Until such arrangements can be effected the most important contribution by far that the rich countries can make to the poor in my opinion is to maintain full employment without (cost) inflation. A steady increase in (the volume of) demand for primary products and the avoidance of periodic monetary shocks—these are the preconditions for lifting the pressure on the terms of trade of the less developed countries. (The attempt to restrict the production of export commodities would in many cases—of which Colombia is an outstandingly depressing example—probably work disastrously against the small producer by favouring the large planters and feudal lords. In any case export producers will almost always be privileged by comparison with the subsistence peasant.)

Nor is this all: for without full employment it would be quite impossible to liberalize the imports of manufactures or (labour-intensive) components. An impressive plea has been made in favour of such liberalization, even if such a course entailed serious unemployment in this or other major industrial countries. However well meant or morally admirable this plea, I fear that, in a democratic country at any rate, such a course would be politically inadvisable, not to say wrong. From an economic point of view, moreover, it neglects the fact that a sudden crisis in an important (labour-using) industry in a fully developed country will have a secondary impact on imports. Now we know from experience that such a recession is likely to affect the price of primary products (the main export items of the less developed areas) far more than the price of manufactures. Thus, while in these matters it behoves us to be very cautious, it is at least not unlikely that such a move might hurt the developing countries indirectly far more than it would help them directly to increase exports, since primary products comprise a very high proportion of their total exports, whereas manufactures are relatively insignificant.

There is a further important argument. The stimulus to the exports of manufactures from less developed countries would redound mainly to the advantage of the urban population, including skilled workers in manufacturing industry, who are in any case highly privileged in relation to the unskilled urban (and much more numerous rural) masses.

The plea of aiding the less developed countries by means of trade liberalization, to the extent that it carries with it the threat of unemployment in fully developed countries, therefore would not in fact achieve the aim claimed for it. Thus the British Labour Party's policy declaration, in emphasizing the primary importance of restoring full employment, is both economically sound and morally justifiable. The British 'liberal' view, on the other hand, amounts simply to an inefficient method of subsidizing the developing countries at the expense of the unemployment of relatively poor and unprotected workers in the more developed countries.

6. UNIT OF ACCOUNT AND INTERVENTION CURRENCY

Much play has been made of the alleged impossibility of the United States devaluing the dollar. We have seen, however, that, far from this being the consequence of some physical peculiarity springing from the dollar's position of unit of account or intervention currency, this is a complete delusion, given credence by the reluctance of the American authorities to buy foreign exchange aggressively. There has been similar misunderstanding concerning the asymmetry of the effects of wider parity margins on the dollar and the rest of the world's currencies.

We have seen that the dollar became the world unit of account almost automatically and that it has also served as intervention currency because of the overwhelming strength of the United States,[15] and because the United States was a creditor on a vast scale with the result that its currency was acceptable to everyone. Dollars were consequently scarce, and they were convertible into gold (or rather until, say, the early 1960s, gold had value because it was convertible into dollars at a price fixed by the U.S. Congress). It is only too likely that, with the end of the Vietnam war, the strength of the dollar will return, especially if the United States takes steps to discourage or control capital movements—at any rate towards other industrial countries. Only if the present success of President Nixon's 'unorthodox', 'arbitrary' and 'totalitarian' measures against cost inflation leads that egregious politician to listen to the siren-song of the conservative Keynesians and monetarists, turn another 180°, and abolish the regulation of prices and incomes, can we expect the crisis of the (abundance of the) dollar to continue.

The so-called devaluation of the dollar in terms of gold, that is in terms of *official* gold, compensated somewhat for the depreciation of gold and S.D.R.s in terms of actual purchasing-power. Inasmuch as most of the less well endowed countries, or those that tried to co-operate with the United States in maintaining an orderly exchange market, possessed only small gold and S.D.R. reserves, this is hardly adequate compensation. On the other hand, a necessary remedy of this defect would be a guarantee of dollar holdings in terms of S.D.R.s. Accordingly, and at any rate as long as the dollar-abundance lasts, the *numéraire* of the system should be denominated in terms of S.D.R.s and the S.D.R.-dollar exchange rate could be altered if price movements in the United States proved overwhelming. This should also end the practice of expressing parities and transactions within the I.M.F. in terms of gold. It is entirely artificial in view of the separation of official gold holdings from the free market. In fact it is hoped that the dollar standard—suitably strengthened by a code of conduct—will once again work satisfactorily, without exporting deflation or inflation. There is no satisfactory alternative in sight.

The problem of the dollar as the currency of intervention has been stated in terms of the snake in the tunnel. Should a currency fall from the top to the bottom of the permitted band and another move from the bottom to the top, the $4\frac{1}{2}$ per cent band *vis-à-vis* the dollar would allow for a movement between the two extremes of 9 per cent. It is argued that this is an unfair advantage in favour of the non-intervention currencies. In fact it is highly unlikely that such violent movements would occur simultaneously. What is more likely is that currencies in the lower range will continue to bob around the bottom and those in the upper range will bump against the ceiling *vis-à-vis* the dollar. If there should then be some pressure in favour of a single currency against both the dollar and other currencies in general—say the yen—then it would be advisable for that currency's parity to be re-valued rather than to adopt the extreme course of floating the dollar (identically with other currencies) against the new *numéraire*. Even under these circumstances it is unlikely that any currency would move the full 9 per cent against the strongest one.

Nor is there any reason to adopt a symmetrical 'multi-currency' intervention system. If the I.M.F. (or its successor) were able to create S.D.R.s for sale to the central bank of the strongest currency, obtaining in return a (non-dollar) intervention currency in order to buy up the weakest currencies, it should be possible then to secure stability within the accepted bands. Alternatively provision might be made for the central banks of both the strongest and weakest currencies to obtain the currencies needed to maintain stability through the I.M.F. The cost of holding reserves, furthermore, could be reduced by providing that S.D.R.s should carry an increased rate of interest, possibly according to a differentiated scale which reflected the relative size of the country's national income and the stability of its exports. A suitable formula could easily be worked out, which might at the same time constitute a further 'link' between international monetary reform and development aid.

If the international monetary system is to function in a balanced way, means must be found by which changes in deposits or drawing rights at the Fund should make themselves felt (as in the case of the gold-exchange standard) as an equivalent change in international liquidity of the creditor countries concerned and thus influence the policy of even the most conventionally minded central bankers. Without this the required balance in the reaction cannot be achieved and it will remain biased against debtors. In my opinion the scheme outlined would achieve such a balance, because the international central bank, in its lending and open-market operations, could insist on 'autonomous' or persistent debtors taking effective remedial action—including, as we have said repeatedly, control over the rate of increase in money incomes—while requiring the same on the part of creditors. In order to do so, however, it must possess powers of sanction, buttressed by the all-round acceptance of the code of good conduct.

7. SANCTIONS

Clearly a system of sanctions, however necessary as an instrument in the hands of the international central bank, must not operate to the detriment of debtor countries alone. It should be possible to extend Keynes's original idea, of shifting an equitable share of the burden of readjustment from debtor countries (who were, if not entirely, the principal victims under the pre-war rules) on to the creditor countries, beyond simple upward parity changes. Thus:

(i) If the creditor country is suffering from unemployment, a variant of the now-defunct scarce-currency clause could be invoked. This might involve the international application of temporary import surcharges or quotas on the exports of persistent creditor countries; these would be maintained until the latter took action to eliminate their current-account surpluses (or rather that portion of such surpluses as were not matched by corresponding exports of capital to less developed areas or by agreed capital exports to industrialized countries) either through expansionary domestic policies or revaluation, or both.

(ii) The degree to which deficit/debtor countries would be permitted to restrict imports from persistent surplus/creditor countries would be related directly to the extent that the latter were maintaining their current-account surpluses by virtue of relatively deflationary policies at home (deliberate unemployment) or to the degree to which they were purposely maintaining an undervalued currency (with less domestic unemployment).

Such a scheme could only be successful, however, if, and only if, the implementation of the code of conduct effectively prevented the deterioration of cost inflation in debtor countries into a hyper-inflation.

An alternative to trade sanctions—and probably more appropriate to cases where a country's export of capital is not covered by a corresponding surplus on current account—would be for the I.M.F. and the central banks of creditor countries to restrict purchases of the currency of the offending (overall-deficit) country to current trade requirements, and hence to permit it to depreciate on a 'parallel market' along French and Belgian lines. Such 'finance' currency, however, must not be available for current-account transactions. As we have said, such controls are difficult to implement. Also, no distribution of S.D.R.s should be made to countries, whether debtor or creditor, which refuse to implement agreed policies for the restoration of balance in international payments. Given a co-operative expansion of world trade, this should be possible without creating unacceptable levels of unemployment.

Finally, however, it is essential also to reassure and safeguard creditors, as an inducement for them to accept such a solution. First, provision could be made for their voting powers to increase as their deposits increased, while stipulating that the further creation of international liquidity would be subject to an affirmative vote by an increasingly qualified majority. Alternatively, the lending power of the international central bank might be limited by some formula, that is, by setting some rate at which liquidity would increase or some relationship between liquidity and aggregate foreign payments. This would be the less desirable alternative, since *mechanical* increases in the *stock* of reserves might not be able to deal with unexpected fluctuations in *flows* (that is, in the balance of payments). This was the real weakness of Professor Triffin's proposals, as against the original Oxford Institute scheme.

8. THE STATUS OF THE NEW INTERNATIONAL INSTITUTION

I think it is Keynes who is credited with saying (after his dreams had been shattered at Savannah) that the I.M.F. ought to have been a bank and the World Bank a fund. The proposed reformed I.M.F. would, in effect, be a central bank. Its proper functioning would demand—as we have seen— far-reaching powers over the general economic, monetary and fiscal, policies of member countries. Consequently it would have to be brought into a much closer relationship with governments and be subject to closer direct control by them than has hitherto, at lease *de jure*, been the case.

No doubt the need for some close co-ordination has been accepted by countries whose policy execution is decentralized (i.e. mainly through the price mechanism). This was the result of historical accident, the quiescence of the I.M.F. during the critical years when the planning and co-ordination of Marshall Aid led to the establishment of the O.E.E.C. (later enlarged, as the O.E.C.D., to include non-beneficiaries and former enemy countries). In fact, had the British bureaucracy shown any initiative, imagination or determination, here was an instrument of inter-governmental (as opposed to supra-governmental) co-ordination with which to establish a consciously controlled development programme, not only for Europe but including the Commonwealth. The ultra-liberal ideals of both the Civil Service and economic advisers coincided with the xenophobia of the public and of politicians of both major British parties. The opportunity of building up a large, and therefore highly complementary, trading area was thus lost. As we have seen, it was left to the central banks to tackle the problems of international co-operation, while the only instruments remaining that were directly influenced or manned by governments were the O.E.C.D. and the annual meetings of the I.M.F. and the World Bank. Even here, the British representative on the Executive Board has never been of high professional standing on economic matters; at best he has been an intellectually brilliant 'generalist' civil servant, with nominations alternating between the Treasury and the Bank of England.

This process must be sharply reversed and the authority of governments over central banks reaffirmed. In order to be effective, however, the structure and personnel of the O.E.C.D. would have to be strengthened. Economists of standing and with government experience should be nominated as government representatives to a much enlarged Economic Committee (the so-called Third Committee) with permanent alternates. This committee should advise the I.M.F. and in certain circumstances suggest policy changes to member governments, possibly on the basis of a qualified vote. For instance, the question of sanctions would certainly fall in the category requiring a qualified majority vote. Also there will need to be a far greater degree of control over the Managing Director of the I.M.F., especially if his experience were to extend to little else besides private or even central banking. Our experience with central bankers has been abysmal, with the outstanding exception of Professor Burns at the Fed and, possibly, Professor Carli of the Bank of Italy, and some of their alternates. (It is to be hoped that the rumour that there have been various intrigues afoot to secure the Managing-Directorship of the I.M.F. for Mr. Jeremy Morse are exaggerated; on the basis of my own experience in Downing Street he would be in no way suited to the task.)

A further requirement, essential for a reorganized I.M.F., is that it should provide for the rotation of the membership of its research department. With time the members of that department inevitably become ensnared and tainted with banking prejudice, and especially with the outpourings of those economic schools which pander to their sense of power by stressing the impact of monetary manipulation. The support given to the revival of monetarist delusions by the I.M.F. (followed by the central banks) serves as a severe warning: under no circumstances should the bankers again be allowed to wreck the world.

Postscript

THE post-1960 oligopolistic struggle should have (but probably has not) taught the world that no monetary reforms can, *per se*, perform miracles— that is, except temporarily. Everybody can be fooled for a time, even about the loss in the real value of money. Monetary reform, however, must, under oligopolistic conditions, imply a certain loss of sovereignty, a certain degree of discretionary disciplinary power and sanction. Hence, supervision of the international agency must be strict and safeguards against abuse stringent. Flexible exchange rates will only 'work' when they are not frequently needed, used or anticipated. The choice is one between compliance with co-ordinating action and the continuation of the oligopolistic struggle in which the strongest impose their will on the rest. As long as the United States was the unchallenged power, economically and politically, its fiat ran (at any rate in the West). Indeed, the United States is still a dominant influence in the world, as was amply demonstrated by the desperate haste with which the Japanese and the Germans took action to prevent a further depreciation of the dollar in 1971–2, and by their unwilling acquiescence in the (entirely justified) American demand for a revaluation of the yen and the Deutsche Mark. A strengthening of the I.M.F.'s powers of reserve-creation is therefore in order, although this would have to be balanced by a closer scrutiny of its measures and rulings.

Recent policy statements in the United States and France would suggest that the comparative victory of the side of reason has not been a permanent achievement. M. Giscard d'Estaing's deflationary package does not differ much from those which Mr. Heath and President Nixon had to abandon amidst public humiliation. Even more disappointing for believers in rational action have been the hints that President Nixon is contemplating abandoning direct controls, despite their undoubted success, in order to convince his bankers of his basic soundness. But it is clear that the forces which created inflation in the United States were not exceptional manifestations of only temporary importance: they remain the outcome of structural change and the inflationary impetus will inevitably recur as soon as the defence measures are weakened, let alone done away with completely.

In international monetary affairs, as in so many other fields, Oxenstierna's dictum applies with a vengeance: it is not merely stupidity, but also short-sighted cupidity, that lies at the root of our discontent.

Notes to Chapters 1–4

1. Cf. T. Balogh, *The Economics of Poverty* (London: Weidenfeld and Nicolson, 1967) ch. 2.

2. For example, cf. J. Viner, *Studies in the Theory of International Trade* (New York: Harper & Row, 1937) pp. 367–74. With the increasing influence of governments over central banks the automaticity of the 'bullion standard' became ever modified. Even Viner tried to take this into account by postulating differences in 'efficiency' in the use of gold. Obviously this afterthought does not account for the phenomena of monetary oligopoly, dominance and bluff, caused on the one hand by policy differences and on the other by differences in reserve positions. It merely meant that a given amount of gold could 'support' a larger volume of credit and payments. Thus, difficulties could still arise from this differential impact on gold flows.

3. Twice in living memory the (very temporary) improvement in the terms of trade of primary-producing countries has prompted economists (even of the standing of Keynes) to express fears of a dearth of primary resources. See, for example, Colin Clark, *The Economics of 1960* (London: Macmillan, 1942). Their discomfiture did not deter economists from predicting famine in the less-developed areas in the 1960s; more recently, however, (often the same) economists are to be heard proclaiming with hosannas the Green Revolution as the solution to the world's food problem. Now, of course, the latest fashion is to forecast global doom in spite (if not because) of these developments (as, for instance, in the utterances of the so-called Club of Rome *et hoc genus omne*).

4. That is, full employment, perfect competition, increasing costs, given tastes, and independence of the terms of trade from policies pursued. Lately Professor Little has again resuscitated this approach which has been so often controverted, cf. I. M. D. Little and J. A. Mirrlees, *Manual of Industrial Project Analysis in Developing Countries* (Paris: Development Centre of the Organization for European Co-operation and Development, 1968) ii, *Social Cost Benefit Analysis*. For a lengthier discussion of the subject cf. T. Balogh, *Unequal Partners* (Oxford: Basil Blackwell, 1963) i, sect. 1, and F. Stewart and P. Streeten, 'Little–Mirrlees methods and project appraisal', *Bulletin of the Oxford University Institute of Economics and Statistics*, **34** (February 1972) pp. 75–91.

5. While it was acknowledged that the 'social' welfare function depended on income distribution, the implications of this vital qualifying condition were blithely disregarded.

6. Cf. *The Economics of Poverty*, ch. 2.

7. Nothing seems to infuriate true believers in *laissez-faire* more than to have the symmetry of international relations denied in favour of cumulative trends to the advantage of one party. This belief in turn now crops up in some of the more ingenuous schemes for symmetrical and simultaneous exchange-rate adjustment, cf. S. I. Katz, *The Case for the Par-Value System*, 1972, Essays in International Finance, No. 92 (Princeton: Princeton University Department of Economics, International Finance Section, March 1972) p. 19; also J. M. Fleming, *Guidelines for Balance-of-Payments Adjustment under the Par-Value System*, Essays in International Finance, No. 67 (Princeton: Princeton University Department of Economics, International Finance Section, May 1968). Such dis-equalizing processes, moreover, do not come to an end 'naturally' but mainly as a result of purposive government intervention. Equally, post-war history shows that the United States lost her favourable current payments position as a consequence of developments outside the scope of conventional economic theory, see Chapter 3, and T. Balogh, *Unequal Partners*, i, Theoretical Introduction, and Gunnar Myrdal, *Economic Theory and Underdeveloped Regions* (London: Duckworth, 1957).

8. If need be, this could be augmented by fiscal or direct means such as a poll tax or the manipulation of consumer demand in order to create the need for cash (as in Indonesia). The abuses of this system resulted in well-intentioned but ill-serving international conventions prohibiting compulsory labour service for peaceful purposes, but permitting them for 'defence' purposes.

9. The recent revival of the 'freer' trade religion, which attributes even the growing horrors of urbanization to misguided protectionism, shows the unrelenting force of neo-classicism. A comparison of recent economic history with the results of 'liberal' colonialism shows a marked acceleration in growth rates, even on conventional measurements. Some of the cost–benefit studies based on this approach have failed to take into account the non-marginality of projects investigated on the basis of partial equilibrium analysis. Such studies could, of course, take into account the existence of unemployment, increasing returns and other 'non-classical' factors by suitable adjustments to the actual structure of private costs, hence allowing for 'social costs' and other considerations in their investment calculations. But if they do, these modifications—especially their quantification—either reduce the operation to a tautology or, by their arbitrariness, involve political valuations. Again, for an example of recent trends, see Little and Mirrlees, *Manual of Industrial Project Analysis, op. cit.*

10. See also Chapter 3 (1)(a).

11. Cf. Lord Keynes, 'The balance of payments of the United States', *Economic Journal*, 56 (June 1946) p. 185. In this article Lord Keynes did not predict— as Professor Kaldor seemed to assume (see *The Times*, 6 September 1951, p. 21d)—the present dollar-plethora crisis.

Elsewhere on the same page Keynes wrote: 'that the chances of the dollar becoming dangerously scarce in the course of the next five to ten years are not very high. . . .' But those were the years of an actual and acute dollar shortage—a shortage that was relieved by precisely those disciplinary measures and direct controls (far in excess of the Bretton Woods provisions) that I had advocated, including the massive aid programme. Aid granted through the latter, in the shape of the European Recovery Programme, rising to more than $12 billion, was alone three times the size of the American contribution to the International Monetary Fund which could have been drawn over four years. In fact Europe's adverse balance of trade with the United States and Canada alone amounted to $6.1 billion in 1947, that is to say one-and-a-half times the total dollar availability in the Fund, cf. H. B. Price, *The Marshall Plan and its Meaning* (New York: Cornell University Press, 1955) pp. 139 and 162. So much for Lord Keynes's prescience in his last liberal–conservative phase. (The history of post-war international monetary experience is taken up again in Chapter 3.)

Chapter 2

1. For reasons of analytical simplicity the sole exception allowed is of complete monopoly: that is to say, the existence of less than perfect competition in international trade is typically acknowledged by *ex-post* modifications to the analysis which, none the less, leave the fundamental approach unaltered. The implications of allowing for imperfect competition, and particularly oligopoly, in trade and *payments* are ignored. (This is reflected, for instance, in the rather simplistic attempts to formulate policy prescriptions based on conventional efficiency- and welfare-criteria—already on shaky ground, but now transposed to the international sphere—according as domestic distortions or monopoly power in trade are assumed to exist or not.)

2. It should be noted that, even for such unimportant parts of the economy as (say) the market for carrots or turnips, the expansion of demand in response to a fall in price (the downward slope of the demand curve) and its independence of supply conditions (the supply curve) can only be assumed by disregarding the historical circumstances of that market and, hence, the likely consequential pattern of anticipations (cf. J. Bhagwati and H. G. Johnson, 'Notes on some controversies in the theory of international trade', *Economic Journal*, 70 (March 1960) pp. 74–93). The proud assertion that bygones are bygones in economic matters is certainly untrue: they co-determine the future and render simple views about economic relationships dangerously misleading. Once these complications are admitted, the simplicity of timeless equilibrium vanishes, even in such restricted cases.

3. Cf. F. D. Graham, 'The theory of international values', *Quarterly Journal of Economics*, 46 (August 1932) pp. 601–2; J. Bhagwati and H. G. Johnson, *op. cit.*

4. Yet such is the strength of conventional opinion that doubt as to the legitimacy of such schedule-mongering succeeds only in being ridiculed as proof of hopeless ignorance. The most absurd of current exercises has been the so-called Phillips curve, the intention being to rehabilitate the neo-classical model within a framework of varying levels of unemployment.

5. Dr. Lamfalussy has recently reiterated this traditional view. 'First, the system must ensure the proper working of the adjustment process, i.e. the spontaneous return to balance of payments equilibrium whenever there is a disturbance. Simultaneously, the system should provide a stimulating framework for adequate adjustment policies, should the spontaneous adjustment process be too slow to work. "Adequate" or "proper" mean in this context processes or policies which cost as little as possible both to the country in imbalance and to the rest of the world.' See *New Currency Solutions and their Implications for Business*, Proceedings (London: Financial Times, February 1972) p. 21.

6. The effects of which were instanced by the 'liberalization' of the Indian textiles industry in the early nineteenth century. It is significant that those who are most in favour of Britain's entry into the Common Market are also those most under the spell of these hoary theoretical fallacies. Alternatively it must be their fervent hope that the Community's 'rules of the game' will help to solve such awkward problems as cost-push pressure without the need to resort to unpopular domestic intervention.

7. These admissions were more in evidence in earlier writings, such as those of Edgeworth, Marshall and Wicksell, than in those of their followers.

8. Professor J. H. Williams's famous essay 'The theory of international trade reconsidered', *Economic Journal*, 39 (June 1929) pp. 195–209 (reprinted in American Economic Association, *Readings in the Theory of International Trade* (1966) pp. 253–71), was a striking exception to this neglect. It also showed that in a 'night-watchman' State even inter-regional differences might be startling: a warning that was almost completely ignored.

9. While there have been some interesting exceptions, e.g. Hong Kong, Singapore and Taiwan, they are numerically trivial. See my reply to Professor Samuelson (1948), 'Static models and current problems in international economics', *Oxford Economic Papers*, N.S., 1 (June 1949) pp. 191–8. Professor Myrdal in his *Economic Theory and Underdeveloped Regions* (London: Duckworth, 1957) called this the 'backwash effect'.

10. The emergence of such products invalidates price and productivity comparisons as a measure of relative superiority. Had the Americans continued to lead rather than follow the world in car production, their 'superiority' might have been maintained, despite unchanged productivity statistics.

11. The fact that Britain was a large *net* beneficiary of change might explain why this did not penetrate classical writings during the unchallenged reign of British economics. The speed with which knowledge spreads among highly industrialized countries has increased, and the monopoly profits of

the dominant area decreased. But the increase in the rate of invention has largely offset this advantage and the discrepancy between industrialized and non-industrialized countries has increased considerably.

12. I have treated this problem in a paper 'The dollar crisis revisited', *Oxford Economic Papers*, N.S., 6 (September 1954) pp. 243–84, in response to Professor Hicks's 'Inaugural lecture', *Oxford Economic Papers*, N.S., 5 (June 1953) pp. 117–35, where he tried, in my opinion irrelevantly and unsuccessfully, to deal with this essentially dynamic problem in a totally static framework. Professor Johnson's taxonomy suffers from similar shortcomings (cf. H. G. Johnson, *Money, Trade and Economic Growth* (London: George Allen & Unwin, 1962) ch. IV).

13. In the sense of not merely overcoming labour-scarcity, but of actually creating technological unemployment: they may also be applicable to a hitherto very labour-intensive industry (such as office machinery, calculators or textiles) far down the scale of previously advantageous items, cf. T. Balogh, 'Factor intensities of American foreign trade and technical progress', *Review of Economics and Statistics*, 37 (November 1955) pp. 425–7, and M. V. Posner, 'International trade and technical change', *Oxford Economic Papers*, N.S., 13 (October 1961) pp. 323–41. The relative volatility of primary-product prices, in combination with this asymmetry, produces disconcerting displacement effects. None the less a great deal of ingenuity has been shown by a number of authors in explaining the so-called Leontief Paradox within the framework of a static equilibrium system: cf. W. Leontief, 'Domestic production and foreign trade: the American capital position re-examined', *Proceedings of the American Philosophical Society*, 97 (September 1953) pp. 332–49; W. Leontief, 'Factor proportions and the structure of American trade: further theoretical and empirical analysis', *Review of Economics and Statistics*, 38 (November 1965) pp. 386–407; for further discussion, together with ample bibliographies, see P. B. Kenen, 'Nature, capital and trade', *Journal of Political Economy*, 73 (October 1965) pp. 437–60, and R. Vernon, 'International investment and international trade in the product cycle', *Quarterly Journal of Economics*, 80 (May 1966) pp. 190–207.

14. The steel industry in India certainly had a comparative advantage, yet in the absence of steel-using industry it was not established—and when established not expanded commensurately with its advantages, cf. T. Balogh, 'The concept of a dollar shortage', *Manchester School*, 17 (May 1949) pp. 186–201.

15. The rapid spread of knowledge would increase risk in the highly developed countries—if the poor countries had the capital and entrepreneurial capacity to exploit that knowledge. In a particular sense this might be thought to be happening in the weaker firms within the 'strong' countries as a result of the activities of the great multi-national corporations which can use cheap labour to both technical and wage advantage in less-developed areas. The repatriated surpluses then increased the degree of oligopoly and profits in the strong countries.

16. Cf. A. Marshall, *Money, Credit and Commerce* (London: Macmillan, 1923) p. 177, and J. Bhagwati and H. G. Johnson, *loc. cit.*, p. 74.

17. See F. Y. Edgeworth, *Paper Relating to Political Economy* (London: Macmillan, 1925) ii, p. 32.

18. The definition of long-run equilibrium is itself nonsense in the context, because of the inseparability of growth and trade. Hence, much of the static principle of comparative advantage or cost loses its validity unless restated in dynamic terms, in which case it would lead to very different conclusions (cf. T. Balogh and P. P. Streeten, 'The inappropriateness of simple "elasticity" concepts in the analysis of international trade', *Bulletin of the Oxford University Institute of Economics and Statistics*, 13 (March 1951) pp. 65–77, and 'Exchange rates and national income', *ibid.* (April 1951) pp. 101–8). This point of view was even accepted by so neo-classical an economist as the late Professor Sir Dennis Robertson: 'There is a large volume of foreign trade trembling, as it were, on the margin of advantageousness, and liable to be blown to one side or the other of that margin by small changes in the wind of circumstance'; cf. D. H. Robertson, 'The future of international trade', *Economic Journal*, 48 (March 1938) p. 8.

19. On the attractiveness of this arrangement for London, cf. *Unequal Partners*, i, Theoretical Introduction, and ii, sect. 6, No. 21.

20. As exemplified by the British position in 1948–9. Larger gold reserves or steadier nerves in the use of controls would have enabled Britain to stay on the old parity until recovery in the United States 'justified' its economic 'soundness'. As it turned out, Britain's Labour government was forced into devaluation. The competitive advantage thus secured, however, was rapidly lost in the violent price-boom of the Korean war and the government's recklessly conceived rearmament plans. The second Labour devaluation in 1967 (as we shall see) also worked slowly and with a serious loss of income.

21. I have attempted to deal with some of these issued in *Unequal Partners*, ii, sect. 5 and 6, and in my essay, 'The dollar shortage once more', *Scottish Journal of Political Economy*, ii (June 1955) pp. 149–56.

22. See *Unequal Partners*, i, sect. 1, and *The Economics of Poverty*, sect. 1.

23. Including the colonial Currency Boards, which had a 100 per cent coverage. The implications of this arrangement for the development of these territories cannot be discussed here, but cf. T. Balogh, 'A note on the monetary controversy in Malaya', *Malayan Economic Review*, 4 (October 1959) pp. 21–26.

24. For example, cf. *International Currency Experience* (League of Nations, 1944).

25. It is, of course, possible even for a diversified exporter to be in an oligopolistic relationship with other countries, on account of its exceptional importance.

26. In the circumstances, therefore, it is just not the case that 'the par-value system has the unique adaptability to offer the authorities a policy option through which the external balance can always be made consistent with measures of domestic balance', S. I. Katz, *The Case for the Par-Value System*, 1972, Essays in International Finance, No. 92 (Princeton: Princeton University Department of Economics, International Finance Section, March 1972) p. 8.

27. This analysis, first put forward in an essay entitled 'Exchange-rate "flexibility"' and economic theory' (*International Currency Review*, 2 (January–February 1971)), has been fully vindicated by the events of the last crisis, and especially by the great difference in the actions and reactions of the various members of the world payments system, in particular the United States and Britain.

28. The British devaluation of 1967, for instance, has proved the 'elasticity-mongers' completely wrong. For example, Mr. Maurice Scott has estimated Britain's price-elasticity of demand for imports of finished manufactures at 7. See M. FG. Scott, *A Study of United Kingdom Imports* (Cambridge: Cambridge University Press, 1963) pp. 43, 100. Mr. Cooper gave it a rather lower value, 2.68, and estimated the price-elasticity of demand for all imports at 0.99 and of foreign demand for British exports at 2.00. See R. N. Cooper, 'The balance of payments' in R. E. Caves (ed.), *Britain's Economic Prospects* (Washington: The Brookings Institution and London: George Allen & Unwin, 1968) ch. 4, p. 189. In a recently published paper, however, the staff of the National Institute present a much less optimistic picture of the process of readjustment. See N.I.E.S.R., 'The effects of the devaluation of 1967', *Economic Journal*, 82 (March 1972, Supplement) pp. 442–64. Not only is it made clear that imports behaved 'perversely' (p. 446), but the elasticities for exports are found to have been far less favourable than (even the Brookings study) supposed: 'The implied price elasticity [of demand for imports] is of the order of one-quarter, which is well below the range of figures from one-half to unity which were being used at the time of devaluation. Even more surprising perhaps is the price elasticity for the exports of manufactures of -1.4. This is lower than the figure of 2 quoted which was widely used at the time of devaluation' (p. 463). These conclusions wholly vindicate the arguments of Professor Streeten and myself concerning the inapplicability of the concept of elasticity to such aggregates as exports and imports which are interdependent and co-determined, cf. T. Balogh and P. P. Streeten, 'The inappropriateness of simple "elasticity" concepts in the analysis of international trade', *Bulletin of the Oxford University Institute of Statistics*, 13 (March 1951) pp. 65–77, and 'Exchange rates and national income', *ibid.*, 13 (April 1951) pp. 101–8 (reprinted in *Unequal Partners*, sect. 5, Nos. 13 and 14, pp. 177–200).

29. Cf. National Institute, *op. cit.*, pp. 447–51.

30. Hence the absence of transfer difficulties in the case of United States aid in both peace and war. Thus the Rueff–Ohlin–Keynes discussion took place on a completely fallacious plane (see *Economic Journal*, 39 (March and

September 1929)). The first two entirely ignored (in 1929 of all years) the possibility of a fall in 'world income' induced (or at least aggravated) by the payment of reparations; Keynes, by arguing on the basis of unclear assumptions as to the behaviour of world (and the recipient country's) income, could not defend his thesis, since he had implicitly accepted a static framework. Later on, neo-classical economists (though not Rueff) would angrily deny that they had ever believed in Say's celebrated law in an 'operational' sense; devaluation in Britain did not cause inflation, but it did cause deflation abroad (cf. *Unequal Partners*, ii, Historical Reflections). The vindication of the Keynesian thesis for the *wrong* reasons—the collapse of world monetary demand after 1929—was directly responsible for the utter mismanagement of the German reparations obligation after World War II. The acceptance of the thesis that no reparations should be paid out of current income (and the 'pastoralization' of Germany, by means of dismantling productive capacity for transfer to the victors, having been abandoned, although more because of the cold war than for humanitarian reasons) resulted in the loss of much-needed payments, not only to Britain but also to much poorer areas, from a Germany which after 1955 could easily have afforded it. The political consequences of Mr. Keynes have indeed been calamitous, and not only in the 1930s.

The 'success' of the British devaluation of 1967 after 1970 is mainly attributable to inflation abroad, as is attested by the increase in export volume, despite relatively too rapid a rate of increase in prices and the consequent violent (10 per cent) improvement in Britain's terms of trade. It should be added that the increase in prices might well have increased exporters' sales efforts—not a matter normally taken into account, and another aspect of the neglect of the increasing 'imperfection' of markets.

31. The conflicting claims made by the heads of the United States Federal Reserve System in the 1920s on behalf of their efforts to 'sterilize' the gold inflow in order to preserve a 'new era' of stable prosperity, and the consequential difficulties caused elsewhere by this one-sided distortion of the classical gold-standard mechanism, foreshadowed problems which are still with us. The continued difficulties of Britain, moreover, demonstrate the clash between the need to maintain investment and thus to protect the increase in productivity, and the *modus operandi* of the classical mechanism which works by restricting demand, thus interrupting growth and (in a dynamic world where wages are not 'instantly' in 'equilibrium') imperilling competitive strength. The classical mechanism could only be conceived of as working satisfactorily in a static world; only in such a world, a world without capital accumulation and changes in productivity, will restriction not prove self-stultifying after a short time.

32. This passage, written in 1970, has been confirmed by American policy since August 1971.

33. I still adhere to our original proposals of 1943 in this respect as being the most satisfactory solution all round, cf. *Unequal Partners*, i, sect. 3, No. 3, and ii, sect. 7, No. 23.

34. See Chapter 3 (1)(b). Through the suspension of the convertibility of the dollar, the grave drawback of its being the means of intervention in foreign-exchange markets has, as we shall see, not altogether been eliminated, but made dependent on the holding by foreigners of dollar balances without access to gold: a situation which is certainly not liked by bankers.

35. See Chapter 3 (2)(a).

36. Cf. T. Balogh, 'International reserves and liquidity', *Economic Journal*, 70 (June 1960) pp. 357–77 (comprising, in part, a critique of *International Reserves and Liquidity* (Washington: International Monetary Fund, 1958), upon which this chapter draws material).

37. A 'desirable' level being understood here to mean one which is in the circumstances compatible with, or conducive to, a state of full employment and relative price-stability. Price-stability, in turn, refers to a state of affairs in which there is no anticipation of continuing inflation and, therefore, no continuing acceleration in the rate of inflation. As we shall see, it is possible that the compatibility of these goals can only be assured by direct controls, in addition to some kind of consensus on incomes.

38. In the study cited in note 36 above, the staff of the Fund also advocated competitive restrictive action: 'The fundamental assistance of the Fund is of course of a short-term character mainly intended to bridge the gap, while the countries *themselves* (italics added) take whatever measures may be necessary to restore equilibrium.' Not a word was said about the assistance of the Fund being required for so long as a major creditor country suffers a deflationary bout. The implication is that assistance must be used to give time to the debtor country to take restrictive measures and cut back ambitious development programmes, irrespective of what the *depressed creditor* may, in turn, be doing. This, as we have argued above, must give deflationary bias to the world economy, cf. Balogh, 'International reserves and liquidity', *loc. cit.*, p. 359.

39. Mr. Katz, for instance, seems to take it for granted that deficit or surplus countries cannot, by their action, influence the rest of the world. This, of course, is quite untrue. Nor is it true that there is 'a combination of policies—under either fixed or flexible-rate arrangements—through which the authorities could always achieve both internal and external balance', S. I. Katz, *op. cit.*, pp. 12–13.

40. The franc zone is a tightly knit organism held together by the control of the French Treasury over government expenditure (which it subsidizes) and of the Bank of France over financial and monetary policy.

41. Economically the United States itself is a regional (rather than national) unit whose high complementarity, which automatically reduces dependence on foreign supplies, is further backed by tariff and quota regulation.

42. The limitation of 'flexibility' of exchange rates as an escape route from unemployment and stagnation is taken up more fully in Chapters 3 (2) and 4.

43. This had been accepted by the Bretton Woods Conference, which prohibited the use of borrowing powers at the Fund to sustain capital exports (Art. VI, Sec. 1(a)). The International Monetary Fund subsequently seemed to regard all capital movements as 'balancing' and did not discuss the need to encourage the application of its own Charter. The spirit of the Charter contrasts sharply with the attitude of the Bank of England as characterized by one of its former Directors, Mr. H. A. Siepman (in a letter to *The Times* on 31 August 1959, p. 9f), who regarded control of capital movements as 'futile and mischievous' or worse. The Radcliffe Committee, in its *Report on the Working of the Monetary System* (London: H.M.S.O., Cmd. 827, 1959), was sceptical as to the effectiveness of control (paragraph 728) but did not discuss this (possibly dominant) reason for its failure; it nevertheless advocated its retention.

   As we shall see, the Executive Board of the Fund has since wholly abandoned this safeguard, which Keynes had regarded as fundamental (see Chapter 3 (1)(a)). Ironically it was the dollar-glut and the acquisitiveness of American multi-national companies which led the French ever more stridently to demand exchange-control for the European Economic Community on the *inward* movement of funds which was resulting in the progressive alienation of national assets in exchange for depreciating dollar balances. Dr. Schiller—that Snowdenian throwback to monetarism—after fierce resistance against such interference with 'freedom' seemed later (February 1972) to have acquiesced in the need for such controls only to resign on this issue at the politically most awkward moment for his colleagues. The British Treasury, in typical fashion, opted out and ended the rather weak controls on the inward flow of dollars, as well as on direct investment in the (defunct) Sterling Area and on portfolio investment, see the Chancellor of the Exchequer's Budget Statement, House of Commons, *Official Report*, 21 March 1972, vol. 833, cols. 1350–1. Similarly, the Bank of England did not even consent to lower interest rates so as to lessen the burden of the huge volume of hot money (probably on account of its hankering after global indirect control of the banking system through the monetary circulation). It would be ironic if the Common Market forced the Bank of England to initiate interventionist policies.

44. By 'excessive' in this context one means a rate of inflation that necessitates continuous foreseeable changes in exchange parities; this will depend on the proneness to inflation of those countries that suffer least from inflation and which are in a persistent creditor position.

45. This was already so in the 1920s. When Montagu (later Lord) Norman persuaded Governor Strong in 1927 to lower the New York discount rate in order to ease London's difficulties, the drift towards the stock market crash of 1929 started, cf. Sir Henry Clay, *Montagu Norman* (London: Macmillan, 1957) p. 237.

46. Cf. T. Balogh, 'Productivity and inflation', *Oxford Economic Papers*, N.S., 10 (June 1958) pp. 220–45.

47. This is especially true if one of the international banking centres, whose liabilities constitute the reserves of other countries, were to start trying to

'increase its liquidity' by 'repaying liabilities'. The thoughtless advocacy of increased liquidity for London was one of the danger points in the latter half of the 1950s; the warning of the Radcliffe Committee (*op. cit.*, paragraph 663) against the ill-considered enforcement of repayments was a welcome note. The much-discussed desire—especially on the part of the continental countries—to put an end to the so-called key- or reserve-currency role of both the dollar and sterling will call for the utmost caution from this viewpoint.

48. An alternative would be to hold spare capacity or stocks of commodities.

49. This will, in turn, depend on the character of international financial organizations.

50. This is the justification—from the 'lending' or surplus colonial territories' point of view—of the British colonial currency and banking system. Unfortunately, the investment policy of the Crown Agents for the Colonies (latterly for Overseas Territories) was so unthinkingly mechanical that 'dear money' caused considerable capital losses to these relatively poor territories. It is interesting that the 'new' Commonwealth countries did not change these arrangements for such a long time and that the question of an exchange-loss guarantee was only raised and exacted during the devaluation crisis of 1967–8 when the Basle agreements were arrived at. Even then, a dollar and not a gold guarantee was thought to be sufficient, thus causing further loss to a number of poor countries.

51. The alternative might well have been deflation and unemployment in the United States, with all that would have implied for the rest of the world (and which, indeed, happened in 1949 and 1959–60).

52. Not only post-war, but in the period after 1929. Indeed, the severity of that depression can, to a considerable extent, be explained by the financial crisis which supervened in 1931, and which eventually disrupted even the American banking system and currency.

Chapter 3

1. Cf. T. Balogh, 'The import of gold into France', *Economic Journal*, 40) (September 1930) pp. 442–60. It is significant that the German representative on the League Committee was foremost in opposing expansionist measures owing to the fear of inflation. There are clear similarities between present attitudes and those prevalent in 1929.

2. A short summary of the history of ideas culminating in Keynes's Clearing Union and Harry White's Monetary Fund can be found in T. Balogh, *Unequal Partners* (Oxford: Blackwell, 1963) ii, Historical Reflections and, especially, sect. 7. The hagiographies of Bretton Woods give a completely distorted picture of the problems raised by American insistence on limiting the potential financial liabilities of the United States. American action to emasculate the 'direct' safeguards of the working of the system has lately come home to roost, when a queer turn in world history has transformed the

United States into a persistent debtor, faced with much less understanding creditors than she herself had proven to be in the end. Richard Gardner (a former student of mine) gives a highly biased account of the fight against Bretton Woods in his book *Sterling–Dollar Diplomacy* (Oxford: at the Clarendon Press, 1956), which is exceedingly unfair to the British opponents of the scheme as it emerged. In a recent review of the working of the Bretton Woods system the breakdown of the arrangements in 1947 is completely ignored and the decisive importance of Marshall Aid to European recovery suppressed. See R. Gardner, 'The political setting', in A. L. Keith Acheson, John F. Chant and Martin F. J. Prachowny (eds.), *Bretton Woods Revisited* (Toronto University Press and London: Macmillan, 1972) pp. 20–33. The travesty of contemporary history is complete.

3. The role of Harry Dexter White will never be wholly satisfactorily explained (see *Unequal Partners*, ii, esp. p. 7).

   Keynes's conversion to liberalism, due to his responsiveness to his environment, was complete. Despite the decisive importance of the rise of Empire trade to Britain's recovery after 1933, he contemptuously dismissed the objections to what Hubert Henderson and myself (among the few) considered to be undue liberalization as a desire to 'build up a separate economic bloc which excludes Canada and consists of countries to which we already owe more than we can pay, on the basis of their agreeing to lend us money they have not got and buy only from us and one another goods we are unable to supply' (Gardner, 'The political setting', *loc. cit.*, p. 26). In the end we are about to join another bloc, but within which we shall undoubtedly be unprivileged.

4. The shortcomings of this model have been discussed in Chapters 1 and 2. As we shall see, the proposed European Monetary Union suffers precisely from these same fundamental defects (see Chapter 3 (1)(b)).

5. Cf. R. F. Kahn, *Selected Essays on Employment and Growth* (Cambridge: at the University Press, 1972) ch. 6, p. 119.

6. The disguise of 'borrowing' as 'purchases' of foreign currencies should have guaranteed the unconditional use of the Fund up to the limit of the full quota. In fact this unconditionality was whittled down and confined to the first (gold) tranche.

7. For a discussion of this episode, see *Unequal Partners*, ii, Historical Reflections (pp. 8–10) and sect. 3, No. 6 (pp. 96–98).

8. See the letter from Sir Hubert Henderson to *The Times* (12 December 1945, p. 5e) and his Stamp Memorial Lecture of 1946, 'The international economic problem', in H. D. Henderson, *The Inter-war Years*, edited by Henry Clay (Oxford: at the Clarendon Press, 1955) pp. 377–87. The reaction of the British Establishment to criticism was similar to that against opponents of Britain's return to the gold standard or her entry into the Common Market. For all its vehemence it might have been aroused by some obscene blasphemy.

9. In Britain this was followed after a short interval by an import-deposit scheme—but not without a desperate rearguard action by orthodox officials.

10. Cf. House of Commons, *Official Report*, 25 July 1969, vol. 304, col. 1177.

11. Cf. House of Lords, *Official Report*, 23 May 1944, vol. 131, col. 844. The 'social-democratic' Dr. Schiller, on the other hand, regarded it as an undue interference with the free play of the price mechanism—as if the 'classical' model knew of hot-money flows.

12. The quota of the United States in the Fund was very large and those of all other countries rather small. Thus, even if other countries had drawn large shares of their quotas in dollars, it would have taken a few years for the Fund's store of dollars to be exhausted. Moreover, the United States was in any case entitled to veto drawings of more than 25 per cent of their quotas in any one year.

13. See *Unequal Partners*, ii, pp. 8–9. The whole Final Act was written in what Keynes in private called the Cherokee language.

14. See *International Reserves and Liquidity*, I.M.F. Staff Paper (Washington: International Monetary Fund, 1958).

15. See F. Machlup, *Plans for Reform of the International Monetary System*, Special Papers in International Economics, No. 3 (Princeton: Princeton University Department of Economics, International Finance Section, August 1962, revised edition March 1964), for the best summary and taxonomy of this subject.

16. For example, see UNCTAD, *International Monetary Issues and the Developing Countries*, Report of the Group of Experts (UN.66.II.D2); UNCTAD, *International Monetary Reform and Co-operation for Development*, Report of the Expert Group on International Monetary Issues (TD/B/285). The device could even be used as a counter-cyclical instrument in addition to securing a steady increase in aid, the transfer problem (as against the resource problem) having been solved. (We shall return to this question in the final chapter.)

17. For example, N. Kaldor, 'The sea-change of the dollar', *The Times*, Business News, 6 September 1971, p. 21.

18. With predominantly short-term lending providing the necessary increase in world dollar reserves. This had been the prevailing system before 1914 with London's money and capital markets at the centre, and the revolving fund of acceptance credits at its base.

19. See Chapter 2 (3)(b).

20. Sterling, already weakened before the war, and further weakened as a result of it, was the first to suffer through the insensate liberalization of foreign investment.

21. As invoked by Keynes in his paper 'The balance of payments of the United States', *Economic Journal*, 56 (June 1946) pp. 172–87. With the revival of

the monetarist school, of course, a sudden respectability has been conferred upon this ancient view. It is, needless to say, quite irreconcilable with Professor Friedman's latest position that monetary changes need as long as (or even longer than) two years to make their effects felt. See M. Friedman, 'Have monetary policies failed?', *American Economic Review*, 62 (May 1962), Papers and Proceedings, pp. 11–18. Perhaps Professor Johnson Mark II* will be able to reconcile this thesis with his own Mark I† view. [*Cf. H. G. Johnson, *Inflation and the Monetarist Controversy* (Amsterdam and London: North-Holland, 1972); perhaps it would be more correct to say Mark III if one bears in mind Professor Johnson's 'primitive' or 'vulgar' Keynesian period, to use his epithets (see *Bretton Woods Revisited*, p. 137). †Cf. Johnson, 'Inflation: the text-book gives no answer', *Financial Times*, 14 November 1970, p. 13.]

22. Keynes, *loc. cit.*, p. 185.

23. The official cumulative current-account balance is in fact shown as £1.3 billion. The figure of £3.2 billion is arrived at by adding back government grants which in the United Kingdom accounts are entered as a charge on the current balance (on government account). This has been done to bring the British figures on to a comparable basis with American official statistics, where no distinction has been made until recently between government capital transactions and outright grants, both being subsumed as a single item under capital account.

24. *Economic Report of the President* (Washington: United States Government Printing Office, February 1971), Appendix C, Table C–87.

25. *Ibid.* (Under the new arrangement the current balance for 1965 appears as $4.3 billion (*Economic Report of the President*, January 1972, Appendix B, Table B–87).)

26. This proportion has been falling steadily, however. A decade earlier, in 1960, the figure had been some 20 per cent.

27. By end-1971 liquid assets had fallen to $13.0 billion and liquid liabilities risen to $64.2 billion (I.M.F., *International Financial Statistics* (monthly), various issues).

28. *Economic Report of the President*, January 1972, Appendix B, Table B–1.

29. *Ibid.*, Tables B–64 and B–87.

30. Keynes, 'The balance of payments of the United States', *loc. cit.*

31. T. Balogh, 'The United States and the world economy', *Bulletin of the Oxford University Institute of Statistics*, 8 (October 1946) pp. 309–23 (reprinted in *Unequal Partners*, ii, sect. 5, No. 12, pp. 149–59 (157–8)).

32. This aspect of the dollar problem has been systematically underplayed by the 'neo-classical' school, and especially by the followers of Chicago and Mont Pélèrin, since it would certainly justify, indeed demand, control over capital movements.

33. Of the Group of Ten, comprising Belgium, France, Germany, Italy, Japan, the Netherlands, Sweden, the United Kingdom and the United States. Switzerland was represented as an 'observer', though participated actively, as did Austria on occasion.

34. Originating with the Basle Agreement of February 1961, the central bankers of the Group of Ten instituted a series of temporary 'swap' arrangements which enabled a country whose currency was under pressure as a result of short-term capital movements to swap its own for some other stronger currency, on condition that the transaction be reversed after three months. Later, in 1965, when Britain had exhausted the whole of her swap facility with the Federal Reserve and her Drawing Rights with the I.M.F., new and more flexible facilities were arranged (in September 1965 and June 1966) at Basle under which standby credits were to be renewable after three months.

   Also, there were the so-called General Arrangements to Borrow, inaugurated in 1962, under the nominal management of the Fund. The purpose of these arrangements was that member countries—effectively the Group of Ten—should stand ready to lend their currencies to the Fund when the need arose. Such credits were to be separate from the Fund's normal resources, their aim being to 'forestall or cope with an impairment of the international monetary system' in the event of a member-country's currency becoming scarce in the Fund.

35. The leads and lags of the 'normal' balance of payments are difficult, if not impossible, to differentiate from 'speculative' losses; the encouragement of the latter through recycling and relending activities is disregarded, since it does not fit the Humean model of international payments.

36. The French position in all this is not without paradox. An increase in the price of gold on the scale envisaged (though not, of course, achieved) would enormously relieve pressure on American gold reserves, while the necessary *quid pro quo* of a revaluation of European (and the Japanese) currencies would have the effect of restoring American competitiveness. What better way of clearing the decks for another period of dollar hegemony?

37. This was later to reach almost 100 per cent, even after the official price had been raised to $38 per ounce in March 1972.

38. The attraction of an undervalued currency and the implications of the German revaluations are discussed in Chapter 3(2)(b).

39. It now seems fairly clear that the ardent advocates in the American State Department, such as Mr. George Ball, of Britain's entry into the Common Market were even less aware of the economic implications of their violent commendations than were their British friends.

40. But see Chapter 3 (2)(c) on the impact-effect of devaluation.

41. The opinion of these is severely critical of the 'nationalistic' and 'protectionist' measures of 15 August 1971, which are argued to have been wholly unnecessary. See, for example, C. Fred Bergsten, 'The new economics and U.S. foreign policy', Brookings Reprint No. 231, Washington, D.C., May

1972, reprinted from *Foreign Affairs* (January 1972) pp. 199–222. But bearing in mind that none of America's European partners nor Japan had shown any willingness to talk or to act effectively in mitigating even that part of the U.S. problem for which they might themselves have been held responsible, the American measures, however brusque, were plainly justified. Even Professor Machlup, who expresses his horror at the 'newly imposed or threatened import barriers of the United States', claims that 'the transitional float was a necessary prelude to the required realignment'. F. Machlup, 'International money: the way forward', *The Banker*, 122 (March 1972) pp. 288–9. Floating constitutes an export subsidy or a tariff of *uncertain* magnitude; in terms of trade aggression it is, to an eye unprejudiced by dogmatic liberal notions, more violent and dangerous than a temporary surcharge.

42. It is sometimes asserted that the United States could not have depreciated the dollar unilaterally. This view is entirely without foundation. By printing sufficient quantities of its currency, the United States, just like any other country, could have provoked a devaluation by resorting to aggressive purchases of other key currencies.

43. It is interesting to note that since March 1961 the Mark has appreciated by more than 30 per cent, yet there is little indication that this has blunted the competitive power of the German economy; so much for the view that it was not the deficiencies in Britain's technical and social organization, but the revaluation of the pound by 10 per cent in 1925, which alone had been responsible for the country's inter-war malaise.

44. According to Thirlwall: 'The basic deficit against which Britain devalued . . . was considerably less than in 1964. It was the "market" balance not the "accounting" balance of payments which proved decisive.' A. P. Thirlwall, 'Another autopsy on Britain's balance of payments: 1958–1967', *Banca Nazionale del Lavoro Quarterly Review*, 23 (September 1970) p. 325. It should be said that by far the best possible moment for a devaluation would have been in January 1967 (or perhaps also April 1966) when the availability of unused capacity and a surplus on the current balance would have made it possible to expand exports without undue strain, and the consequent export-led expansion could have put Britain on the way to full employment. Indeed, I had pressed for devaluation at both those times, as opposed to some experts who advocated it in 1964 and in the summer of 1966, both periods of hectic growth.

45. Consumer prices in the United States rose by 3.4 per cent in the year to October 1972, compared with a rate of increase of some 6 per cent per annum during 1969 to 1971. It is interesting to note with what evident approval *The Economist* now reports on President Nixon's policy, when it is recalled how that Journal had always been opposed to it, having advocated deflation pure and simple along with measures to curb the power of the unions. See *The Economist*, 245 (25 November 1972) pp. 55–56.

46. The countries of the Common Market—almost certainly on French insistence —reacted sharply to the widening of the margin of 2¼ per cent on either side

of parities. In so far as this would permit fluctuations of up to 9 per cent between any two currencies (one appreciating the full 4½ per cent from its floor against the dollar, the other depreciating the full 4½ per cent), this was a comprehensible reaction; the Common Agriculture Policy could not have taken the strain. On 7 March 1972 it was therefore agreed by the Finance Ministers of the Six to narrow the overall band within which E.E.C. currencies could fluctuate against each other to 2¼ per cent by 1 July at the latest; thus the 'snake' was to be only one-half the width of the Smithsonian 'tunnel'. In fact the plan was implemented well before the deadline, on 24 April, and Britain joined the scheme on 1 May (having already announced on 15 March her intention to do so). The long-term aim, of course, was still to reduce margins to zero.

47. The pound's new official floor being $2.5471. Furthermore, Britain had managed to remain inside the snake for just about as long as convertibility had lasted in 1947; the lesson had not been learnt.

48. The communiqué issued after the Smithsonian meeting contained, apart from the short-term 'package', the following longer-term proposals: 'It was agreed that attention should be directed to the appropriate monetary means and division of responsibilities for defending stable exchange rates and for insuring a proper degree of convertibility of the system; to the proper role of gold, of reserve currencies, and of special drawing rights in the operation of the system; to the appropriate volume of liquidity; to re-examination of the permissible margins of fluctuation around established exchange rates, and other means of establishing a suitable degree of flexibility; and to other measures dealing with movements of liquid capital. It is recognized that decisions in each of these areas are closely linked.' *The Times*, Business News, 20 December 1971.

49. Moreover, an academic—in contrast to British tradition in the choice of Chancellors of the Exchequer.

50. Statement by the Hon. George P. Shultz, Secretary of the Treasury and Governor of the Fund and Bank for the United States, at the Joint Annual Discussion, International Monetary Fund Press Release No. 21, Washington, D.C., 26 September 1972.

51. One is reminded of one of Keynes's famous passages on the subject of bankers: 'So, if they are saved, it will be, I suspect, in their own despite', *Essays in Persuasion* (London: Macmillan, 1931) p. 178.

52. Efforts on the part of the French to gain support against the linking of monetary and trade negotiations and to secure a unilateral monetary dis-armament by the United States (through the latter's acceptance of the reintroduction of dollar convertibility) are as comprehensible as her own unilateral violation of the Bretton Woods rules on (say) multiple exchange rates: they are, of course, quite illogical. Downward movements in a currency's exchange rate constitute as much a 'tariff' on imports as they do a 'subsidy' on exports, and vice versa with upward movements. To ask for a

freezing of the impact of exchange fluctuations on trade without counter-vailing assurances in the field of tariff and non-tariff barriers is to demand unilateral concessions. It is to be hoped that the Americans will hold out for an equitable settlement. Unfortunately Mr. Nixon's supporters in the United States dislike and distrust pure managed currencies without a firm link with gold; even more do they dislike exchange controls over the expansion of their vast pile of foreign assets. Thus the tactical position of the United States is not as firm as it might have been.

53. Mr. Heath's carefree capitulation or deference to President Pompidou on almost all the major issues (itself explicable only on the basis of similar disregard or ignorance) had the effect of isolating the United States within the Group of Ten and of giving encouragement to the French moves. The Americans, having had enough of the cabals of the Six within the Ten, reacted brusquely and refused to participate in the meetings of the Group of Ten until they had succeeded in widening it to include all the nations represented on the Executive Board of the I.M.F. The French, in answer to this move and to the Americans' refusal to prolong M. Schweitzer's tenure as Managing Director of the Fund, succeeded in frustrating the election of the American candidate to the Chairmanship of the new Committee of Twenty.

54. Cf. Commission of the European Communities, 'Memorandum on the coordination of economic policies and monetary co-operation in the Community', *Bulletin of the European Communities*, 2 (March 1969), Supplement to No. 3.

55. See Article VIII of the Final Communiqué of the Conference of Heads of State or Government on 1 and 2 December 1969 at The Hague (2 December 1969).

56. See, for example, the Schiller, second Barré and Giscard d'Estaing plans. On 6 March 1970, however, the Prime Minister of Luxembourg, M. Pierre Werner, was invited to chair a working party with a view to drafting a report analysing the various suggestions and bringing out 'the fundamental policy choices to be made so that the economic and monetary union of the Community can be achieved by stages'.

57. On the basis of the final Werner Report. See Commission of the European Communities, 'Report to the Council and the Commission on the phased achievement of economic and monetary union in the Community', *Bulletin of the European Communities*, 3 (November 1970), Supplement to No. 11.

58. Though it is questionable as to how far the Summit resolutions can be regarded as an acceleration. In fact the date of the implementation of resolutions of the Ministers of the Community of 26 March 1972 concerning the European Regional Development Fund ran into difficulties in September 1972 in the Council of the Six, and the Summit Conference amplified the remit to the Finance Ministers but postponed its implementation from 1 October 1972 to 31 December 1973 and that of the European Monetary Co-operation Fund from 30 June 1972 to 1 April 1973.

59. The only developed trading countries in Western Europe to revalue their currencies against the dollar by less than Britain were Italy and Sweden.

60. For example, see S. E. Harris (ed.), *The New Economics: Keynes' Influence on Theory and Public Policy* (New York: Knopf, 1948); M. Stewart, *Keynes and After* (London: Penguin Books, 1967); and R. Lekachman, *The Age of Keynes* (New York: Random House, 1966 and London: Allen Lane The Penguin Press, 1967).

61. This is shown by the fact that the wartime fears of economists (myself included) of a repetition of the 1921 slump were proven unjustified, and the counter-measures unnecessary.

62. Or, more strictly, Lord Kahn's earlier appreciation of the elastic response of real output (employment) to a change in (monetary) demand. See R. F. Kahn, 'The relation of home investment to unemployment', *Economic Journal*, 41 (June 1931) pp. 173–98; but see also M. Kalecki, 'A macro-dynamic theory of business cycles', *Econometrica*, 3 (July 1935) pp. 327–44 (first presented at the meeting of the Econometric Society, Leyden, October 1933).

63. Hence the vilification of J. K. Galbraith's *The New Industrial State* (London: Hamish Hamilton, 1967).

64. See J. Tinbergen, *On the Theory of Economic Policy* (Amsterdam: North-Holland, 1952) chs. 4 and 5. But there is, of course, no such 'law' and, like Professor Tinbergen's other discoveries and models, it does not stand up to serious examination. And Mr. Katz, too, can still blithely assert, even in 1972, that there will always be a combination of policies through which to bring internal and external balance into compatibility without seriously considering the possibility that this may require at the same time a radical change in motivations and institutions. See S. I. Katz, *The Case for the Par-Value System, 1972*, Essays in International Finance, No. 92 (Princeton: Princeton University Department of Economics, International Finance Section, March 1972) p. 13.

65. N. Kaldor, 'Conflicts in national economic objectives', *Economic Journal*, 81 (March 1971) p. 3.

66. *Ibid.*, pp. 4–5.

67. *Ibid.*, p. 3.

68. See also T. Balogh, 'Exchange-rate "flexibility" and economic theory', *International Currency Review*, 2 (January–February 1971) pp. 1–10. Professor Kaldor, in a widely misunderstood article (see 'Mr. Heath's new socialism', *Sunday Times*, 8 October 1972, p. 62), has been interpreted as being wholly convinced of the excellence of Mr. Heath's recent package on prices and incomes, acceptance of which 'could usher in a period of social and economic progress exceeding in scale and duration that of any previous era of British history', although he (Kaldor) fills the package with further measures which must be quite unacceptable to a Conservative Prime

Minister. Perhaps a rather less circumlocutory approach to what is an obviously unjust, though nimble, political gambit would have been more felicitous. Nor is Professor Kaldor's current policy-bee (managed floating) absent: even though, in the event of the Heath package (or anything approaching Mr. Wilson's norm) proving acceptable, Britain's balance of payments would show a dramatic improvement, Professor Kaldor would still want to see the pound float—presumably upward. The reason for this is difficult to fathom.

69. At the other extreme the 'modern' monetarists seem to believe that anticipations are stable and stabilizing and that external and internal balance merely requires the strictly proportionate inverse adjustment of the exchange rate *vis-à-vis* whatever the rate of inflation happens to be (the latter, of course, still being wholly attributable to the rate of domestic credit expansion).

70. As long as the oligopolistic element in price determination continues to be disregarded, and as long as mechanical devices such as labour–supply curves (however much these may be tinkered with) are resorted to, 'explanations' of inflation will remain misleading and implausible. Cf. D. Jackson, H. A. Turner and F. Wilkinson, *Do Trade Unions Cause Inflation?*, University of Cambridge Department of Applied Economics, Occasional Paper 36 (Cambridge: at the University Press, 1972).

71. See, for example, the Oxford Symposium on Money and Credit, especially P. P. Streeten and T. Balogh, 'A reconsideration of monetary policy', *Bulletin of the Oxford University Institute of Statistics*, 19 (November 1957) pp. 331–9. This view has been accepted now (October 1972) in an oblique manner by the Bank of England. Faced with the weakness of the pound and the stiffening of interest rates, the Bank rate was simply abolished to avoid the unfavourable psychological impact which attends its increase. (It is as if the peasant were to break the thermometer in order to avoid the fever.) It has been replaced by a 'minimum lending rate' based on the prevailing rate on Treasury bills. As might have been predicted, the rate rose by $1\frac{1}{4}$ percentage points. If other rates rise in sympathy, which is not unlikely when deposits are the object of an oligopolistic struggle, the only result will be an interest-induced cost-plus acceleration in the rate of inflation—until the psychological climate suddenly changes. Should the Bank, on the lines of the Chancellor's statement, ever wish to reintroduce Bank rate, it will be difficult to avoid a panic.

72. The violent swings in the 'propensity' to save caused by sudden waves alternating between hire-purchases and repayments; the increase in the relative importance of durable consumers' goods in total expenditure; these have rendered obsolete the kind of 'models' propounded by Harrod and Hicks, if, indeed, they were ever realistic.

73. This sort of attitude had serious political consequences in Latin America in the late 1950s and culminated in the 1960s. It is also reflected in Mr. Jenkins's Letter of Intent to the I.M.F. (23 June 1969) restricting domestic credit expansion to not more than £400 million in 1969–70.

74. Cf. M. Friedman, 'What Price Guideposts?', in G. Shultz and R. Aliber (eds.), *Guidelines, Informal Controls and the Market Place* (Chicago: University of Chicago Press, 1966) p. 26.

75. Experience all over the world has shown that, in the new industrial systems that rely for their viability on mass production, the needs of productive efficiency in most industries will militate towards a reduction in the number of firms. A concentration of power will inevitably ensue, which will enable entrepreneurs to manage their selling prices within practicable limits which, in turn, will be closely related to movements in wage costs.

76. This is not to say that in some countries inflation was not at certain times the result of excess demand. Britain in 1955, 1959 and 1964 (the Conservative election-boom years), Germany in 1966 and the United States in 1956 and 1966–7 were almost certainly suffering from demand inflation. But this does not detract in the slightest from the overwhelming importance of cost inflation.

77. The abject acknowledgement of this and other failings has in fact become a central theme of Presidential Addresses in recent years at a variety of economic conferences. Cf. F. H. Hahn, 'Some adjustment problems', *Econometrica*, 38 (January 1970) pp. 1–12; W. Leontief, 'Theoretical assumptions and nonobserved facts', *American Economic Review*, 61 (March 1971) pp. 1–7; E. H. Phelps Brown, 'The underdevelopment of economics', *Economic Journal*, 82 (March 1972) pp. 1–10; G. D. N. Worswick, 'Is progress in economic science possible?', *ibid.*, pp. 73–86. It seems unlikely, however, that these open expressions of doubt have altered what econometricians would call the underlying trend.

78. Cf. Friedrich August von Hayek, *Prices and Production* (London: Routledge, 1931) and especially his reply to Straffa's review article, F. A. Hayek, 'Money and capital', *Economic Journal*, 42 (June 1932) pp. 237–49.

79. Cf. P. Straffa, 'Dr. Hayek on money and capital', *Economic Journal*, 42 (March 1932) pp. 42–53 and his rejoinder to Hayek, *ibid.* (June 1932) pp. 249–51.

80. Cf. F. A. Hayek, *A Tiger by the Tail*, Hobart Paperback No. 4 (London: Institute of Economic Affairs, 1972) and G. Haberler, 'Incomes policies and inflation', in G. Haberler *et al.*, *Inflation and the Unions*, Readings in Political Economy No. 6 (London: Institute of Economic Affairs, 1972) pp. 3–62.

81. This was reflected in the disregard for my first pamphlet (*Planning for Progress*, London, 1963) and later in the animosity with which the second (*Labour and Inflation*, London, 1970) was received. Mr. George Brown (now Lord George-Brown) was one of the notable exceptions to have instinctively understood the vital importance of a solution to this problem for Britain's prospects. Subsequently, when the ending of the 'period of severe restraint' in June 1967 had brought in its train the crisis in the autumn of that year and the consequent wage explosion (partly exacerbated by the rise in prices due to increased indirect taxation and higher welfare charges introduced in

the July 1967 measures), Mr. Roy Jenkins was to announce the end of Labour's attempt at an incomes policy almost by way of an aside in his 1969 Budget speech.

82. A. A. Walters, 'A failure of economics?', *United Malayan Banking Corporation Economic Review*, 2, 2 (1971) pp. 27, 28.

83. Cf. M. Friedman, 'A theoretical framework for monetary policy', *Journal of Political Economy*, 78 (March–April 1970) pp. 193–238.

84. Cf. M. Friedman, 'Have monetary policies failed?', *American Economic Review*, 62 (May 1972) Papers and Proceedings, pp. 11–18.

85. Mr. Katz (*op. cit.*), though, has not yet moved. But, of course, he was presumably writing some twelve months ago and, if the efforts of financial journalists are anything to go by, twelve weeks are enough to produce secular changes in theoretical attitudes.

86. Cf. G. D. N. Worswick, 'Prices, productivity and incomes', *Oxford Economic Papers*, N.S., 10 (June 1958) pp. 246–64.

87. Cf. National Institute of Economic and Social Research, *Economic Review*, No. 60 (May 1972) p. 14.

88. Cf. Conservative Manifesto, *A Better Tomorrow* (London, 1970) p. 13.

89. Much the same, though less starkly, can be said of President Nixon's first years in office; unlike Mr. Heath, however, he was goaded by the inflexibility of the American electoral cycle. Thus, at electorally almost the last moment, he made a brisk about-turn and attempted to attain internal balance by means of a policy of price and income guidelines.

90. Between June 1970 and June 1971 the rate of inflation of retail prices rose from 5.9 to 10.3 per cent per annum; while by December 1971 the index of industrial production was only 0.6 per cent higher than in June 1970.

91. The number of wholly unemployed (excluding school-leavers) rose from 669,300 to 859,000 in calendar 1971 to reach a peak of 917,600 in March 1972.

92. In the year ending June 1972 domestic credit expansion measured £4374 million, compared with £955 million and £268 million during the two preceding four-quarterly periods.

93. Cf. House of Commons, *Official Report*, 21 March 1972, vol. 833, col. 1354.

94. By July 1972 the rate of inflation had fallen to 5.8 per cent, but by September it had risen to 7.0 per cent.

95. There are, however, certain voices that advise us to approximate the Latin American condition and to learn to live with inflation by adjusting all or most incomes to rising prices. For example, cf. H. G. Johnson, *Inflation and the Monetarist Controversy* (Amsterdam: North-Holland, 1972). Like previous pleas for liberal fiscal and monetary policies and for floating

exchange rates, this too is pernicious. Latin American dictatorships can no doubt maintain their ignominious existence under the pretence of stability; these countries, however, are riven between rich and poor, the former never investing in money assets, the latter never having anything to invest anyway. It is inconceivable that a democracy of Britain's standing should follow or be expected to follow such advice.

96. In the case of the electricity workers' dispute in Britain in the winter of 1970–1, the social ostracism to which they were spontaneously subjected was an important element in the agreement eventually reached.

97. See Joan Robinson, *Essays in the Theory of Employment* (London: Macmillan, 1937) for a vivid description of these.

98. Cf. R. N. Cooper, *Currency Devaluation in Developing Countries*, Essays in International Finance, No. 86 (Princeton: Princeton University Department of Economics, International Finance Section, June 1971) pp. 28–31. (Interestingly enough, Professor Cooper seems since that time to have rediscovered the problems caused by the income effects and secondary reactions attendant on the devaluation of an important currency—factors long ago discussed by Mr. Streeten and myself in *Unequal Partners*, i, sect. 5, Nos. 13 and 14).

99. Including the British Government between 1926 and 1929 and the governments of the countries of the Gold Bloc after 1933.

100. As the balance of payments of the United States went the way of Britain's, the Americans began increasingly to complain that the Bretton Woods system contained a devaluation-bias against them. Since the dollar was the intervention currency and *numéraire* of the system, the United States could only alter its exchange rate by persuading its competitors to revalue themselves or by entering the market and bidding aggressively for foreign currencies at new levels. (Both courses were distasteful and fraught with the threat of a trade and currency war.) There is nothing in this, however, that is intrinsic to the dollar's position as intervention currency *per se*, but rather in the overwhelming industrial strength of the United States which the rest of the world would wish to keep in check with the help of an overvalued dollar.

101. This pattern was reinforced in Germany when the Deutsche Mark was devalued in 'sympathy' with sterling in 1949.

102. Dr. Schiller's deflationary Budget proposals in 1972 and his subsequent resignation suggest that that classical monetarist might have arrived at the end of his road.

103. Cf. T. Balogh, 'The United States and international economic equilibrium', in S. Harris (ed.), *Foreign Economic Policy for the United States* (Cambridge, Mass.: Harvard University Press, 1948) pp. 446–80; also H. Henderson, 'The function of exchange rates', *Oxford Economic Papers*, N.S., 1 (January 1949) pp. 1–17, and R. F. Kahn, 'The dollar shortage and devaluation', *Economia Internazionale*, 3 (February 1950) pp. 89–117, reprinted in R. F. Kahn,

Selected Essays, ch. 2, pp. 35–59. It is regrettable that fallacies long ago exposed should so easily succeed in being revived. Not only does it reveal the shallowness of those claims which economists are in the habit of making for the scientific nature of their profession, but—more important—it inhibits progress in the understanding of economic matters.

104. Report by the High Level Group on Trade and Related Problems to the Secretary-General of O.E.C.D., *Policy Perspectives for International Trade and Economic Relations* (Paris, O.E.C.D., 1972).

105. Report by the Executive Directors to the Board of Governors of the I.M.F., *Reform of the International Monetary System* (Washington, D.C.: I.M.F., 1972).

106. Statement by the Hon. George P. Shultz, I.M.F. Press Release No. 21, 26 September 1972.

107. Cf. M. Parkin, 'An overwhelming case for European monetary union', *The Banker*, **122** (September 1972) p. 1140.

108. *Ibid.*, p. 1142 (all italics in original).

109. Cf. R. G. Lipsey and M. Parkin, 'Incomes policy: a reappraisal', *Economica*, **28** (May 1970) pp. 115–38.

110. See T. Balogh, *Labour and Inflation* (London: Fabian Society, 1970) pp. 63–64, and L. Godfrey, 'The Phillips curve: incomes policy and trade union effects', in H. G. Johnson and A. R. Nobay (eds.), *The Current Inflation* (London: Macmillan, 1971) pp. 99–124.

111. Cf. S. I. Katz, *op. cit.*

112. For a representative sample of the strangely outmoded manner in which the whole subject of international adjustment and monetary reform is discussed see: Report of Working Party 3, *The Balance of Payments Adjustment Process* (Paris: O.E.C.D., August 1966); C. Fred Bergsten *et al.*, *Approaches to Greater Flexibility of Exchange Rates: the Bürgenstock Papers* (from Princeton: Princeton University Press, 1970); S. Marris, *The Bürgenstock Communiqué: a Critical Examination of the Case for Limited Flexibility of Exchange Rates*, Essays in International Finance, No. 80 (Princeton: Princeton University Department of Economics, International Finance Section, May 1970); and T. Willet *et al.*, *Exchange-rate Systems, Interest Rates, and Capital Flows*, Essays in International Finance, No. 78 (Princeton: Princeton University Department of Economics, International Finance Section, January 1970).

113. P. Jay, *The Times*, Business News, 4 February 1972. This is a handsome acknowledgement of the newly discovered limitation of a change in parities by a writer who ascribed the failure of the Labour Government to a refusal to devalue in 1964—when, incidentally, he had been an ardent supporter of the Treasury's hostility at that time to both devaluation and the reinforcement of exchange control.

114. N.I.E.S.R., 'The effects of the devaluation of 1967 on the current balance of payments', *Economic Journal*, 82 (March 1972, Supplement) pp. 463–4.

115. *Policy Perspectives* . . ., *op. cit.*, p. 35, para 124.

Chapter 4

1. I have set out my views on this in 'A new view of the economics of international readjustment', *Review of Economic Studies*, 14, 2 (1947) pp. 82–94 and in 'Exchange depreciation and economic readjustment', *Review of Economics and Statistics*, 30 (November 1948) pp. 276–85, reprinted in *Unequal Partners*, i, sect. 3, Nos. 6 and 7.

2. For example, Sir Roy Harrod, who has recently accepted that traditionally 'deflationary' Keynesian measures may be price-inflationary, omits devaluation from his list. Cf. Sir Roy Harrod, 'Problems perceived in the international financial system', in *Bretton Woods Revisited*, *op. cit.*, p. 15. There is no doubt, however, that the economics profession is slowly but surely coming to an awareness of the problem. Thus, as is admitted in the *London and Cambridge Economic Bulletin*: '. . . there is only limited past evidence on the response of exports and imports to depreciation of the exchange rate. More important, any devaluation will add to inflationary pressures on domestic costs which will reduce the effectiveness of the devaluation itself. The calculations ignore this feedback effect because it cannot be quantified and, since they are constructed on manifestly artificial assumptions, must be treated as illustrative. *In reality devaluation is probably an even less effective remedy than is shown here.*' *The Times*, Business News, 9 January 1973 (italics added).

3. See note 48 of Chapter 3.

4. See page 42.

5. Cf. M. Kalecki, F. Schumacher and T. Balogh, *New Plans for International Trade* (Oxford: Blackwell, 1943) and *The Economics of Full Employment* (Oxford: Blackwell, 1944).

6. *Unequal Partners*, i, sect. 5, No. 13.

7. We have seen that Sir Roy Harrod seems to have perceived this danger although the upholder of current orthodoxy, in the inflated shape of Professor Johnson, resorts as usual to denunciation rather than argument in his criticism of this view (*Bretton Woods Revisited*, p. 137). Yet once anticipations are admitted, the 'vulgar' or 'primitive' Friedmanite view also becomes non-operational.

8. Cf. J. M. Keynes, *A Tract on Monetary Reform* (London: Macmillan, 1923) p. 190.

9. French insistence that a country whose currency is under attack should repay the assistance provided by its E.E.C. partners (and eventually by the European Monetary Fund) in gold or convertible currencies rather than dollars is yet another rather unsuccessful attempt to displace the dollar as an intervention currency and to enforce discipline on debtor countries. In both aims they necessarily failed and had to consent to the use of dollars.

10. T. Balogh, 'Old fallacies and new remedies: the S.D.R.s in perspective', *Bulletin of the Oxford University Institute of Economics and Statistics*, 32 (May 1970) p. 98.

11. Cf. *Unequal Partners*, i, sect. 6, No. 19.

12. Cf. G. Haberler, 'Prospects for the dollar standard', *Lloyds Bank Review*, No. 105 (July 1972) pp. 1–17.

13. The principal cause of malaise has been the exceptionally low mortality rate which has led to a rapid acceleration in the rate of population growth.

14. Discussed above, Chapter 4 (1).

15. See, for example, *Economic Survey of Europe in 1971* (New York: United Nations, 1972), Part I: *The European Economy from the 1950s to the 1970s*, p. 3.

Index

Printed in Great Britain by Hazell, Watson & Viney Ltd. Alyesbury.